REMOTE WONDERS

REMOTE WONDERS

An Explorer's Guide to Southeast Oregon

MELVIN R. ADAMS

WSU PRESS

Washington State University
Pullman, Washington

WSU PRESS

Washington State University Press
PO Box 645910
Pullman, Washington 99164-5910
Phone: 800-354-7360
Fax: 509-335-8568
Email: wsupress@wsu.edu
Website: wsupress.wsu.edu

First printing 2015, Second printing 2023

Library of Congress Cataloging-in-Publication Data

Adams, Melvin R., 1941- author.
Remote wonders : an explorer's guide to southeast Oregon / Melvin Adams.
pages cm
Includes bibliographical references.
ISBN 978-0-87422-332-3 (alk. paper)
1. Oregon—Guidebooks. 2. Historic sites—Oregon—Guidebooks. 3. Oregon—Description and travel. 4. Oregon—History. 5. Natural history—Oregon. I. Title.
F874.3.A33 2015
917.9504—dc23

2015018744

Dedicated to my father—Millard Adams

What makes a desert beautiful is that somewhere it hides a well.
—Antoine de Saint-Exupery

Coyote is always out there, and he is always hungry.
—Navajo proverb

I would rather wake up in the middle of nowhere
than in any city on earth.
—Steve McQueen

Contents

Acknowledgments

I would like to thank Gene Pierson, Andy McDonald, and Mike Hagood for offering constructive comments on the manuscript. It is a better book because of their thoughtful efforts. I would also like to thank John Fulton and his family for road testing the map and manuscript during their trip to southeastern Oregon. Thanks, too, to my grandson Marty and his father Matt for road testing the manuscript with me on a trip to eastern Oregon. Their comments were most helpful. I also want to acknowledge the entire staff of WSU Press, including Beth DeWeese for her patient and diligent efforts editing the book.

Introduction

OREGON'S REMOTE CORNER is a vast, open land of grass, sage, basalt rims, and dry lakes. East of the Cascade Range, the region borders California, Nevada, and Idaho. Some five hours by car from temperate Portland, and encompassing Lake and Harney Counties, and parts of the surrounding counties, the climate is semi-arid, and some areas are high, cold deserts. To the person driving through, it can seem uninteresting and barren, with only a few ranches and towns along the way. But to those who take the time to look and study it carefully, it is a topography of wonder with a history of human perseverance. It is a landscape worthy of consideration and reverence.

This book highlights a variety of locations that will give the traveler a good introduction to the natural and human history of southeastern Oregon. Listed in general clockwise order, beginning and ending in Burns, Oregon, featured sites show evidence of early Native American inhabitants and reminders of turn-of-the-century ranching empires, U.S. government efforts to pacify tribes living in the region, timber processing, and gold mining. Other sites showcase geology, volcanos, past climates, playa lakes, fossil beds, and habitats where only extremophiles such as lichen, brine shrimp, and diatoms can live in wind, brine, ice, and heat. A map inserted in the back of the book is provided to guide travelers along the way. The remote quarter is sometimes referred to as a high desert, a steppe, the Oregon desert, or the Oregon Outback. I use these words interchangeably.

Rich in natural and human history, Oregon's remote corner can be seen as a microcosm of the American West. Here is an opportunity to learn a great deal about the history of the West and its flora, fauna, geology, mineralogy, atmosphere, and climate. Part One of the book is devoted to specific locations of interest, while Part Two highlights selected geology, flora, fauna, and atmospheric phenomenon travelers are likely to see. The appendices include a proposed trip plan, hazards and how to avoid them, side trips, a comparative historical timeline, and a checklist for children. I know that people exposed to this part of Oregon either love it or hate it. It is my hope that this book will encourage people to love it as I always have.

An Explorer's Tour of Oregon's Remote Corner

AT THE BACK OF THE BOOK you will find a removable map of Oregon's remote corner. Featured sites summarized below are indicated on the map in red with numbers keyed to the chapter numbers in the book. A quick scan of this list will introduce you to the highlights of history and nature you'll find as you travel through this remarkable region.

Summary of Featured Sites		
Chapter	Site	What to look for
1	Pete French Round Barn	Late 1800s ranch architecture, history of an Oregon cattle empire.
2	Diamond Craters	Variety of volcanic features in a reltively small area including maars (craters).
3	Steens Mountain	Fault-block mountain. Heavily glaciated terrain with cirques, tarns, hanging valleys, moraines, and other glacial features. "Sky island" habitat for flora and endemic species including Skinner's Sulfur butterfly, Steens Mountain paintbrush, and Steens Mountain thistle.
4	Malheur Refuge	Important nesting and resting area for many migratory species of birds.
5	Malheur Cave	Very large lava tube cave with endemic albino species.
6	Borax Lake and Tum Tum Lake	Natural and mineral hot springs hosting extremophile species. View of east facing escarpment of Steens Mountain.
7	Shirk Ranch	Early ranch architecture and history of an early cattle empire.
8	Long Lake	World-class petroglyph site. Hard to access.

9	Greaser Petroglyph	Petroglyph boulder on list of National Register of Historic Sites. Easy to access.
10	Stone Corral and Warner Lakes	Chain of lakes and wetlands at base of Hart Mountain escarpment. Important habitat for waterfowl. Historic rock corral left from early ranch.
11	Stone Bridge and Camp Warner	Important petroglyph and military history site.
12	Sunstone Collection Site	One of few sites open to the public for collecting Oregon's state gem.
13	Petroglyph Lake	Well-documented petroglyph site on the Hart Mountain National Antelope Refuge. Look for pronghorn antelope, mule deer, and bighorn sheep. Lake is typical of a vernal pool.
14	Lake Abert and Chandler State Park	Classic pluvial lake in horst and graben topography at the foot of the Abert Rim escarpment. Important wildfowl habitat due to high concentrations of brine shrimp and brine flies. Artifacts of the Chewaucan culture. Explored by John C. Fremont. Old-growth ponderosa pine grove nearby at Chandler State Park.
15	Alkali Lake	Example of a playa lake. Nearby shorelines show evidence of old pluvial lake. Look for greasewood flats and iodine bush. Home of endangered Hutton Tui chub. Burial site of Agent Orange-related waste chemicals.
16	Willow Ranch and Goose Lake	Ranch was an active sawmill and box factory site for several decades. Sawmill artifacts including wood burner and log raft boats. Area is a microcosm of the historic stages of the American West including exploration, pioneer era, ranching, mining, sawmilling, resorts, orchards, railroads, and finally abandonment.

17	Lily Lake and High Grade Mines	High mountain, eutrophic lake, glacially cut near the summit of the Warner Range. Dragonfly hot spot. Abandoned gold-rush-era mining structures.
18	Dog Lake	Biologically productive lake in the Fremont National Forest.
19	Chewaucan River	High desert river restored for native redband trout.
20	Gearhart Mountain	Differentially eroded geological features; high mountain lake, springs, meadows, aspen and ponderosa pine groves, and glacial features. Look for bear, mountain lions, pika, and dippers.
21	Sycan Marsh	Important bird resting and nesting area restored by the Nature Conservancy. Site of native trout restoration projects.
22	Cottonwood Meadows	High mountain lake with nearby skunk cabbage meadow. Look for beaver and cougar.
23	Summer Lake Hot Springs and Summer Lake Refuge	Natural hot springs historic mineral pool. Refuge is a restored wetland and a world-class location for viewing migratory and nesting waterfowl and shore birds. Historic ranch structures and farming implements on display.
24	Slide Lakes	Geologically unusual lakes formed by large landslides. Drowned Ponderosa pine trees and floating log gardens; good fishing. Road to lakes provides excellent views of Summer Lake and Winter Ridge. Look for native wild plums and wildflowers near small waterfalls tumbling out of the mountains.

25	Fort Rock	Volcanic tuff ring. Caves nearby were important in dating early human occupation of North America. Nearby park contains buildings and artifacts from the homesteading era.
26	Lost Forest	An anomalous ponderosa pine forest resulting from a unique soil substrate. Site of some of Oregon's oldest and largest junipers. Nearby dune field is one of largest in state. Look for rare green-tinged paintbrush.
27	Glass Buttes	An important site for a wide variety of obsidian.

Please note that if the map is missing from this book, replacements are available for $3 from Washington State University Press, PO Box 64510, Pullman, WA 99164-5910, wsupress@wsu.edu.

PART ONE
Places and History

Pete French Round Barn

1. The Round Barn ❧ Pete French

A VISIT TO THE FIVE-ACRE Pete French Round Barn State Heritage Site provides a look at an early Oregon cattle empire and a remnant of historic ranch architecture. Pete French was born in Missouri in 1849, then raised on a sheep ranch in the Sacramento Valley. As a young man, he left his father's ranch to work for Dr. Hugh Glenn, a wealthy California rancher and wheat farmer. Glenn eventually sent French north with 1,200 head of cattle, some vaqueros, and a Chinese cook to find new grazing lands. French arrived at the Catlow Valley, recognized the fine grazing land, and acquired from a man named Porter a small herd and land rights in the Blitzen Valley on the west side of Steens Mountain. French's P Ranch became the nucleus of a vast cattle empire in eastern Oregon.

Pete French built fence lines, bunkhouses, line cabins (cabins far removed from the main ranch for use by the cowboys who rode distant fence lines to make repairs and round up strays), and a headquarters on the Donner and Blitzen River. With financial help from Glenn, French acquired land at rock bottom prices via the Swamp and Overflow Act, which transferred swamp lands from federal to state ownership to be drained for agricultural use. He grew meadow hay, broke hundreds of horses, and built irrigation works. French married Glenn's daughter in 1883, and Glenn was murdered a short time after by a disgruntled former employee. French managed the Oregon ranch for the Glenn heirs, forming a partnership called the French-Glenn Livestock Company. (Frenchglen is a small town and school near the former P Ranch headquarters.) French ultimately controlled over 200,000 acres of land and ran 45,000 head of cattle.

In June 1878 Paiutes and Bannocks attacked the P Ranch. They burned structures, shot a horse out from under French, ran off cattle, stole horses, and killed one of French's men. The attacks continued throughout the summer. In the arid and semi-arid west, disputes over water rights and boundaries sometimes led to violence. In such a dispute between French and rancher Ed Oliver, French was killed. A charge of murder was made against Oliver, but he was found not guilty.

Probably the most interesting artifact remaining from the P Ranch cattle empire is the round barn. The Pete French Round Barn is the only one remaining of three similar barns that were built on the ranch to break horses during the tough winters. Between three hundred and one thousand horses were trained every year in the P Ranch barns.

The barn interior consists of a circular wall made of local rock and mud enclosing the central stable area. The remainder of the building is made from lumber brought in from sixty miles to the north. The roof is supported by a large, central juniper post. Around the outside wall is a circular covered track for working the horses in the winter.

Historically, round barns could be octagonal, polygonal, or circular in plan. The octagonal era lasted from 1850 to 1900, with the circular era overlapping somewhat from 1889 to 1936. The years 1880 to 1920 were the peak of round barn construction in the United States. The Pete French round barn was probably built sometime in the late 1870s to early 1880s, placing it before the heyday of round barn construction.

The barn was donated to the State of Oregon by the Jenkins family in 1969 and placed on the National Register of Historic Places in 1971. A visitor's center near the barn includes a small museum and a gift shop with a wide selection of books, western apparel, gifts, and food items for sale. The round barn can be reached by way of Highway 78 southeast from Burns and hence south from New Princeton and is not far from Diamond Craters and the historic Hotel Diamond.

2. Diamond Craters

According to one geologist, "Diamond Craters has the best and most diverse basaltic volcanic features in the United States and all within a comparatively small and accessible area" (Benedict 1985). Designated an Outstanding Natural Area by the Bureau of Land Management (BLM), Diamond Craters—near the Malheur National Wildlife Refuge—abounds with geologic features including grabens, ash-flow tuff, driblet spires, spatter rings, a maar, craters, lava tubes, a shield volcano, kipukas, cored bombs, pyroclastics, pahoehoe lava, fissures, breadcrust bombs, scoria cones, and a caldera, all of which are defined and described in the chart below. It is particularly unusual to find such varied features in one place. (Information for the table was derived in part from Benedict 1985 and Bates 1957.) A self-guided tour map is available from the Bureau of Land Management, Burns District Office, www.blm.gov/or/districts/burns.

Malheur maar, also known as Diamond Pond

Geologic Features at Diamond Craters

Feature	Description	Diamond Crater Example
Ash-flow tuff	Rock formed from consolidation of a highly heated mixture of volcanic gases and ash. Tuff is a general term for all consolidated pyroclastic rocks.	Devine Canyon Ash-flow Tuff—a weathered reddish-brown layer of ash and rock.
Breadcrust bomb	A volcanic rock with a checkered and cracked exterior resulting from expansion of the interior. A bomb is a blob of lava ejected while viscous and shaped while in flight.	Red Bomb Crater.
Caldera	A circular, basin-shaped volcanic depression.	Central Crater Complex.
Cored bombs	Marble- to baseball-sized rocks caused by explosions of magma that rise through water-soaked layers then are blown out by steam and cool in the air. Some have glassy cores.	Big Bomb Crater.
Crater	A basin-like structure on a cone formed by explosion or collapse.	A crater or craters are found throughout the area.
Driblet spires	Thick globs of molten lava that have spouted a few feet into the air and plopped down to stack up around a spout.	Lava Pit Crater.
Fissure	A crack, break, or fracture in rocks and flows.	Northeast Dome features deep, numerous, parallel fissures. Some are 40 feet deep, 8 feet wide, and 250 feet long.
Graben	An elongated, depressed block that is bounded by faults along its sides.	Graben Dome has a main graben and two smaller grabens at right angles. The main graben is 100 feet deep, 7,000 feet long, and 1,250 feet wide.

Feature	Description	Diamond Crater Example
Kipuka	A kipuka is an area of land surrounded by younger lava flows.	Big Bomb Crater.
Maar	A broad crater formed by hot magma coming in contact with ground water. The crater often fills with water. Sometimes defined as a feature made when no magma surfaced during the explosion.	Dry Maar and Malheur Maar. Malheur Maar is water-filled. Also see East Twin Crater.
Pahoehoe lava	Hawaiian term for basalt lava flows with a smooth or ropy texture as opposed to a rough, jagged texture (aa lava).	Central Crater Complex.
Pyroclastics	A general term for solid material of any size ejected from a volcanic vent into the air.	Found throughout Diamond Craters.
Scoria cone	A cone made of cinders that are vesicular (containing small cavities) due to the escape of volcanic gases before solidification. Scoria is heavier, darker, and more crystalline than pumice.	Red Bomb Crater.
Shield volcano	A broad, gently sloping volcanic cone of flat conical shape built of overlapping basaltic lava flows.	Lava Pit Crater.
Spatter ring	A ring built by lava fountains around a vent. It is usually basaltic material.	Graben Dome.
Tephra	A general term for all clastic materials (rock fragments) ejected from a volcano and transported through the air. Includes volcanic dust, ash, cinders, scoria, pumice, and bombs.	Tephra is found throughout Diamond Craters in various forms.

One of the more interesting features of Diamond Craters is Malheur Maar, also known as Diamond Pond. Scientists have studied Diamond Pond using core sampling to determine micro- and macro-fossil composition, sediment types, pollen content, and plant grains, and radiocarbon analysis to date specimens (Wigand 1987). The research established a record spanning the last 6,000 years that revealed long-term climate changes in and near the pond, including changes in water levels and plant communities. Researchers have found evidence of severe drought between 2,900 and 500 years ago. The pond is one of the most significant desert lakes between Mexico and Canada for studies of past climates and for shedding light on global climate change.

Diamond Craters is accessible via Highway 205 south from Burns or via Highway 78 south from New Princeton. It is convenient to also visit the Pete French Round Barn State Heritage Site when visiting Diamond Craters.

3. Steens Mountain

STEENS MOUNTAIN IS THE largest fault-block mountain in the northern Great Basin, and offers views of numerous geologic features, diverse vegetation, and unusual birds and animals. Thirty miles long, with a summit nearly 10,000 feet high, Steens Mountain was named after army major Enoch Steen who fought the Paiute Indians in the area. Today the mountain is managed as the Steens Mountain Cooperative Management and Protection Area.

The Great Basin is a physiographic province—or geographic region—consisting of many parallel fault-block mountains and ranges extending over much of Nevada, the western half of Utah, California east of the Sierra Nevada, a small portion of Idaho, and the southeastern quarter of Oregon. Named deserts in the Great Basin include Black Rock Desert, the Great Salt Lake Desert, the Sevier Desert, the Smoke Creek Desert, the Mojave Desert, and part of the Sonoran Desert. The Great Basin has internal drainage with no outlets to the sea. Most of the Great Basin is arid or semi-arid, and is typical of horst and graben topography.

Steens Mountain was heavily glaciated during the Pleistocene Era and glaciers carved five deep, U-shaped canyons on the mountain. (The only other glaciers in southeastern Oregon were much smaller, including small examples on the Warner Mountains and Gearhart Mountain.) Drainage from the canyons on the gentle, west-facing slope of the mountains gives rise to four Wild and Scenic Rivers: Donner and Blitzen, Wildhorse, Little Wildhorse, and Kiger. The canyons display a number of features common to glaciated topography, including cirques and tarns. A cirque is the amphitheater-like basin formed at the head of a valley glacier by erosion. If the cirque contains water to form a lake due to damming by glacial deposits (moraines) or other causes, the lake is called a tarn.

Steens Mountain is made primarily of basalt that was laid down in multiple flows some sixteen million years ago. Studies of Miocene lava flows at the mountain show patterns in magnetic crystals in the lava that document the reversal of the earth's magnetic poles 780,000 years

Glacial-cut gorge on Steens Mountain

View from Steens Mountain summit looking east into Alvord Basin

ago (Brown 2000). The Steens basalt rests over Steens Mountain andesites, the Alvord Creek beds, and the Pike Creek volcanic beds. The Alvord Creek beds exposed on the eastern scarp are made of water-deposited volcanic material and contain fossil evidence of twenty-six species of late-Miocene plants including six species of conifers that are largely absent from the Steens Mountain today. The Pike Creek formation features colorful shades of pink and reddish-brown rhyolite but also contains andesites, dacites, thunder eggs, quicksilver, and uranium ore.

From the summit of the mountain, the fault block drops precipitously more than a mile into the Alvord basin. The rain shadow of Steens Mountain means that the Alvord basin gets only about seven inches of rainfall per year. The dry lake of the Alvord desert was, during the glacial Pleistocene Era, covered by three hundred feet of water by ancient Lake Alvord. Wave-cut shorelines are visible on the slopes above the basin. Many large lakes occupied the Oregon Outback during the Pleistocene—including Lake Chewaucan, which once encompassed present day Summer Lake and Lake Abert—leaving similar shoreline patterns on slopes throughout the region.

The Alvord Basin has geothermal springs and pools resulting from groundwater heated by underground magma. Some of these are suitable for bathing including Alvord Hot Springs. Mickey Hot Springs features the only bubbling mudpots in Oregon.

Steens Mountain is known as a "sky island" because it supports plants and animals known from widely separated areas. Biologists have described five vegetation zones there: desert scrub in the Alvord Basin; a staircase of sagebrush, juniper, and aspen as elevation increases on the western slope of the mountain; and an alpine bunchgrass tundra zone on the higher parts of the mountain. These zones support a wide variety of flora and fauna. The Alvord sand dunes are home to more than 1,100 species of arthropods and 80 species of plants. A distinct population of Skinner's Sulphur butterfly on the mountain feeds on dwarf huckleberry. Sixteen species of boreal animals, including the pika, live on Steens Mountain. Eleven reptiles and twenty mammals have been found in the Alvord Desert Area of Critical Environmental Concern. The streams, lakes, and ponds of Steens Mountain and the Alvord Basin host a number of uncommon, rare, threatened, or endangered fish species: Lahontan cutthroat trout, Malheur mottled sculpin, Borax Lake chub, Catlow tui chub, Alvord chub, Catlow Valley redband trout, and Great Basin redband trout. Larger animals in the area include bighorn sheep, Pronghorn antelope, elk, and mule deer.

The flora of Steens Mountain is unusual in many respects (Mansfield 1995). There are 1,115 species of vascular plants including 57 listed in the Oregon Biodiversity Center's *Rare, Threatened and Endangered Plants and Animals of Oregon* (orbic.pdx.edu/documents/2013-rte-book.pdf). Botanists expect to find forests of Douglas fir, ponderosa pine, and Engelmann spruce on the mountain but they are not present. The absence of subalpine conifers may be a result of the isolation of the mountain—the sky island effect. However there are small groves of Sierran white fir in two drainages—another apparent anomaly. There are six varieties of plants endemic to the mountain including Steens Mountain paintbrush and Steens Mountain thistle.

Restoration efforts on the north side of Steens Mountain are focused on preserving sagebrush steppe and microbiotic crust, and could be beneficial throughout the Great Basin and the Columbia River basin (Brown 2000). Efforts include cutting junipers, which shade out grazing grasses and reduce groundwater levels; controlled burning; and aerial reseeding. While big sagebrush has declined some 99 percent in the Columbia River basin, Steens Mountain supports a variety of sagebrush and steppe types through a range of elevations. This provides habitat for the sage grouse—a species that is of concern throughout the Oregon Outback.

Perhaps the most efficient way to become familiar with Steens Mountain is to stay at the Frenchglen Hotel or the restored Hotel Diamond in Diamond. The Malheur Wildlife Refuge is at the foot of the western slope of the mountain. From the Frenchglen Hotel, a visitor can cross the Donner and Blitzen River and drive the north loop road ascending to the summit. The road is usually open after July 4, and is sometimes washboarded but passable. Those driving SUVs can complete the loop from the summit to the south; about eight miles of this road is steep and rocky and not suitable for passenger cars. Notable places to stop on the north loop include Lily Lake, Fish Lake, and Jackman Park. On this loop the traveler will see spectacular U-shaped glacial canyons, aspen groves with the carvings of Basque sheepherders still visible on the bark, mountain meadows, high mountain lakes with floating lily pads, and spectacular views into the Alvord Basin from the summit. Lily Lake is at a more advanced stage of eutrophication than Fish Lake. As a lake matures it begins to fill in with sediments and plant debris and eventually becomes a meadow. Many of the meadows on the mountain were once lakes or ponds. Fish Lake provides opportunity for some high mountain trout fishing, while camping is available at Jackman Park.

Travelers should be careful driving the higher reaches of the loop, particularly right after the snow melt. The road may be open, but the mud can be formidable. My first job after college was teaching science at Burns High School. During a memorable field trip, my students and I had to push a school bus out of a mud hole on the top of Steens Mountain. Visitors should be aware of sudden changes in weather at the summit. Once when coming out of Little Blitzen Gorge on horses, we saw cumulus clouds building up below us. (Yes, the mountain is high enough that weather builds up below.) Before long we were in a full-scale thunder and lightning storm on the exposed summit. I was ready to believe in Zeus that day.

4. Malheur National Wildlife Refuge

The Malheur National Wildlife Refuge consists of 185,000 acres of open water, marshes, irrigated meadows and grain fields, riparian areas, and uplands. The refuge rests at the foot of the western slope of Steens Mountain. Since prehistoric times the Malheur and Harney Lakes have hosted vast flocks of migratory birds on the Pacific Flyway. By the late 1800s, pioneer settlers and then plume hunters from the millinery trade began to decimate the populations of swans, egrets, herons, and grebes. Drainage of the wetlands also reduced the habitat of the birds. Concern for the survival of these species and others led President Theodore Roosevelt to issue an executive order in 1908 establishing the refuge protecting the Malheur, Harney, and Mud Lakes for bird habitat. In 1935 the P Ranch was added to the refuge.

The P Ranch land of the original Pete French cattle empire is at the heart of the refuge today. The long barn, a beef wheel (a wooden wheel

Narrows at Malheur Lake

used to hoist beef sides for cooling and curing), and some fences still remain from the P Ranch era, along with the Pete French Round Barn. The lakes, ponds, and wetlands of the refuge are fed by the Donner and Blitzen River that originates in the Steens Mountain via snowmelt. Since the refuge is part of the Great Basin, there is no outlet of the water from the basin.

The refuge supports 320 bird species and 58 mammal species. The open water attracts white pelicans, loons, terns, grebes, and gulls. The marshes nourish trumpeter swans, Canada geese, ducks, and sandhill cranes. Other nesting species include ibis, several species of egrets, herons, sandhill cranes, and Franklin's gulls.

The seasonal round of birds on the refuge is well described in the Malheur Refuge brochure, which is available at the refuge headquarters or online at www.fws.gov/Malheur. The brochure lists the species likely to be seen at the various ponds and overlooks on the main refuge road. The following lists the location of some of the most interesting birds on the refuge.

Buena Vista Ponds and Overlook

- Red-wing blackbirds
- Yellow-headed blackbirds
- Trumpeter swans
- Cinnamon teal
- Ruddy duck
- Gadwall
- Great Blue heron
- Black-crowned night-heron
- Barn swallows
- White pelicans

Benson Pond

- Orioles
- Great-horned owl
- Pied-billed grebe
- Migrating warblers
- American coot

P Ranch

- Loggerhead shrikes
- Audubon warblers
- Red-tailed hawks
- Marsh wrens
- Sandhill cranes
- Tree sparrows

Knox Pond (closed March 1–August 1)

- Sandhill cranes
- Ibis
- Franklin's gull
- Ringneck pheasant

The George Benson Memorial Museum at refuge headquarters has on display a collection of some two hundred mounted specimens of local birds. This and other buildings on the refuge were constructed by the Civilian Conservation Corps in the 1930s. Reach the refuge by way of Highway 205 south from Burns. Nearby sites to visit include the Pete French Round Barn, Steens Mountain, and Diamond Craters. Find historic lodging accommodations and food at the nearby Frenchglen Hotel or the Hotel Diamond. Campgrounds near Frenchglen include Page Springs and Camper Corral.

5. Malheur Cave

MALHEUR CAVE, southeast of New Princeton, is a classic example of a lava tube. A lava tube forms when a lava flow cools on the surface and develops a hard insulating crust that allows the lava underneath to keep flowing.

Malheur Cave is 3,000 feet long and varies from 8 to 20 feet in height. The lower end of the cave is filled with water, creating an underground lake. The underwater portion of the cave has been mapped by divers (Hill 2000). Among the artifacts found on the floor of the lake were three boats and, alas, a great deal of trash. Underground springs introduce water that is clearer and warmer than the main body of water in the cave.

Inside the dry portion of the cave are wooden bleachers and a wooden podium used by the Masons who own the cave. The cave is open to visitors.

Evidence that the cave was used by Indians and early settlers includes obsidian chips (lithic scatters) and soot stains on the walls from fires. An Indian legend told by Captain Louie—a Paiute chief who died in Burns—told of the cave being used by the Paiutes as a defensive position against attacking Bannocks. In the legend, Coyote warned the Paiutes of the impending attack of the Bannocks and the Paiutes took food and water into the protection of the cave. The Bannocks attempted to starve them out and shot hundreds of arrows into the mouth of the cave but finally they broke off the attack. Coyote told the Paiutes when it was safe to come out.

The cave is home to some interesting arthropods. The Malheur Cave Springtail (*Oncopodura mala*) is a small (one to six millimeters in length), unpigmented hexapod (six-legged insect) with an appendage called the furcula extending from the end of the abdomen that enables it to leap and escape predators (Christiansen and Bellinger, 1996). Other specimens have been collected from caves in California. Springtails feed on decaying plants, algae, and bacteria. They molt up to fifty times but do not put on much additional growth.

Another arthropod in the cave is Hubb's amphipod (*Stygobromus hubbsi*). This is a medium-sized, carnivorous type of crustacean similar to cave species in California. This species feeds on bacteria in the water and the species type *hubbsi* is found only in Malheur Cave.

I visited Malheur Cave in the 1960s and saw albino, eyeless fish, but I have been unable to find any documentation that others have seen them.

6. Borax Lake ❧ Tum Tum Lake

BORAX LAKE is a geothermal lake located on the southern end of the Alvord Desert to the east of Steens Mountain, about six miles northeast of the town of Fields, Oregon. The lake is approximately ten acres in size with an average temperature of 86° F (Furnish 2002). Cyanobacteria and diatoms live in the lake along with 296 species of invertebrates. The most diverse group is the *Diptera* (true flies) with 84 species (Furnish 2002). Borax Lake may host the last remaining population of the lamb rams-horn aquatic snail as well as being the only known habitat for the Borax Lake chub. The chub was listed as endangered under the Endangered Species Act in 1982.

Most of the lake is about three feet deep but a vent at a depth of more than one hundred feet discharges hot water that mixes with the lake water. The lake sits on the crest of a biomorphic mound composed of diatoms, silt-size silica particles, mineralized plant fragments, and plant and charcoal layers (Cummings et al. 2010).

The water of Borax Lake has a high concentration of dissolved solids (about 1,600 milligrams per liter) consisting of sodium, bicarbonate, sulfate, and chloride. There are also concentrations of toxic metals like arsenic, cadmium, cesium, copper, lead, and mercury occurring at much higher levels than in seawater (Furnish 2002). High concentrations of iron and silicon support diatom growth. Near the lake are salt tolerant plants such as shadscale, alkali saltgrass, and greasewood.

In the late nineteenth century the Rose Valley Borax company bought the springs and the land around it and mined it for borax salts for ten years. Wagons pulled by mules transported the borax to a railroad in Winnemucca, Nevada. The mining ended in 1902. Some ruins of buildings from the mining period can still be seen near the lake.

Borax Lake is one of the best places in the state to observe dragonflies, including a number that are not found anywhere else in Oregon (Kerst and Gordon 2011). Among the butterflies at the lake are the Comanche, Bleached and Hoary Skimmers, Desert Whitetail, Paiute Dancer, Alkali Bluet, and Black-fronted Forktail.

Borax Lake's unusual microbiology, flora, fauna, hydrochemistry, and thermal geology have attracted considerable attention from scientists. In order to protect this fragile area, the Nature Conservancy bought 160 acres of private land including Borax Lake, and the Fish and Wildlife Service designated 640 nearby acres as critical habitat. The area has also been designated off limits to geothermal development and mining.

Tum Tum Lake is located about nine miles south of Fields, Oregon, at the foot of the Pueblo Mountains. The lake covers approximately 1,500 acres and was designated a Research Natural Area by the BLM to protect a salt desert shrub community. The lake is also habitat for the Alvord chub, designated as a "special status" species under the Endangered Species Act. Three special status plants in the area include iodine bush, salt heliotrope, and verrucose seapurslane. Tum Tum Lake can be accessed via Highway 205.

7. Shirk Ranch

House at Shirk Ranch

FROM 1883 TO 1914, David Shirk and his brother William operated a ranching empire in the Guano Valley in the Oregon steppe south of the present day Hart Mountain National Antelope Refuge. The ranch is now owned by the federal government and the remaining buildings are listed on the National Register of Historic Places.

The Shirk brothers began ranching in the Catlow Valley in what is now Harney County. Later they acquired the Guano Valley ranch to raise horses. The Catlow Valley ranch was the scene of a number of Indian attacks during the Bannock War of 1878. William and two teamsters were once ambushed and the two teamsters were killed but Shirk escaped. The ranch was about 50,000 acres and controlled much of the water in the area, which led to conflicts with Pete French's P Ranch. During a land claim dispute in 1889, David shot and killed one of French's workers. Shirk was tried for murder but was not found guilty. By 1899 the Guano Valley ranch was expanded to 1,080 acres.

Today the David L. Shirk Ranch Historic District includes the main house, two bunkhouses, a blacksmith shop, a wood shed, an outhouse, a chicken coop/animal shed, a water tower, two wells, original fences, a dam and irrigation system, and a grave site. The most interesting structures are the main house and the water tower.

The circa 1910 main house is on a stone foundation and has shiplap siding and a gable roof. It was used by ranchers until the 1980s. Today the house has greatly deteriorated under the ownership of the BLM.

The two-story water tower was also built about 1910. The lower exterior walls were covered with rubble stone. A galvanized metal water tank was on the second floor supported by log joists and log posts. The irrigation system features a low earth-berm dam faced with hand-placed stones. Ditches channeled water to the meadows south and east of the ranch.

A grave marker northwest of the main house testifies to the violent history of the West. The headstone says, "Here lies Bill Vickers and J. Gruenke, Shot August 14, 1887." The details are a mystery but it was rumored that two bank robbers stumbled onto the ranch and were quickly dispatched.

In his book, *The Cattle Drives of David Shirk: From Texas to the Idaho Mines, 1871 and 1873,* David Shirk recounted many anecdotes about ranching on the wild eastern Oregon frontier. For example, in July 1878 word reached David Shirk from his brother that the "Bannack" (sic) Indians had gone on the "war path" and were headed for the "Stein Mountain" (sic) country. At the time Shirk was in the field with his wife, his wife's sister, and another woman friend. They hastened to return to the Home Creek ranch. One day at dawn his wife cried out, "Why don't you shoot?" as some riders approached. Shirk recognized the riders as his Chinese cook and some of the "boys." "I had never seen my wife so excited," recalled Shirk. "And as she was an expert with the rifle the only wonder is that she did not open fire on the approaching men... Mrs. Shirk was one of the bravest little women I ever knew, and the fact that she was then carrying her first baby probably accounted for her excitement." Soon after, Shirk and his family learned that Pete French and his men were attacked by Indians and their cook was killed in the fray.

The Shirk brothers were among the original cowboys on the trails of the West. When they arrived in Oregon they found a cattlemen's paradise with bunch grass growing up to the bellies of their horses. But in the end the paradise could not be sustained and the once beautiful ranch house and water tower now slowly deteriorate in the desert sun and wind.

Shirk Ranch corral and sagebrush

8. Long Lake

ONLY EXPERIENCED DESERT TRAVELERS should attempt the trip into the Long Lake site. A high-clearance vehicle with strong tires (ten ply) is recommended to navigate the rocky, almost nonexistent road. There is a real danger of breaking a tire on sharp rocks or getting high centered on rocks and damaging the vehicle's oil pan. Someone may have to go ahead on foot to throw rocks out of the road. There is no cell phone service. The road can only be negotiated at a speed of one to two miles per hour. There is no potable water, so be prepared for a dry camp.

But the trip has its rewards. Long Lake is a world-class site for petroglyphs—prehistoric rock carvings. The two-mile-long rim rock is covered with petroglyphs for almost its entire length. Near the south end on top of the rim rock is a small circular stone site with a petroglyph. I believe that some of the petroglyphs at Long Lake and nearby sites refer to the supernova explosion of 1054 that created the Crab Nebula. Astronomers have documented other possible depictions of this event in the Southwest and at Lava Beds National Monument (California). The panels depicting this event at Long Lake are somewhat more sophisticated in that they appear to also enumerate the number of days the supernova was visible during the daytime. There are also a number of other important petroglyph sites around Long Lake (see Loring and Loring 1996).

Long Lake is remote and lonely. There are no nearby lights, the sky is clear, and the atmosphere thinner due to the elevation of the site, making it an idea place to appreciate the Milky Way and the abundance of stars in the sky.

Long Lake is east on Highway 140 from Adel, Oregon. Check with the BLM office in Lakeview for routes into the area. On the way to Long Lake, be prepared to see animals including antelope, mule deer, coyotes, mountain bluebirds, and sage grouse.

9. Greaser Petroglyph

Greaser Petroglyph boulder

IN THE OREGON DESERT most petroglyphs are carved on smooth faces of basalt rock, on boulders, or rim rock. Petroglyph sites in the Oregon steppe include Long Lake, Stone Bridge, Sheep Creek Spring, Petroglyph Lake, and Rabbit Creek to name a few (Adams 2002). There are 248 documented sites in Oregon, most of them in the eastern and particularly the southeastern parts of the state (Loring and Loring 1996; Cressman 1937). One of the most astonishing is the Long Lake site (Adams 2001). There, more than 1,300 petroglyphs are scattered along a two-mile long, fifteen-foot high rim face and on boulders at the foot of the rim. Petroglyphs at Long Lake have been dated to 6,600 years BP by virtue of the fact that some of them were buried under Mount Mazama ash from the eruption that formed Crater Lake National Park. However, parts of the Oregon desert have been occupied for 14,000 years or more, which suggests that some of the petroglyphs could be older than 6,600 years.

Petroglyphs were made by pecking, drilling, abrading, or scratching the rock face. Pictographs, or painted drawings on rock, also appear on the basalt but they are more susceptible to weathering and are found in more protected locations.

The meaning of petroglyph symbols is a topic of discussion among archaeologists, with a number of different hypotheses about their purposes and meanings. I have studied the petroglyphs of the Oregon desert for some twenty years, and have discovered some sites not previously documented. I therefore offer my theory of the meaning of the petroglyphs—a theory that is shared by at least some archaeologists (Turpin 1994). About 80 percent of the petroglyphs can be explained with reference to the shamanic trance flight cycle sometimes called a vision quest. The shaman enters into a trance flight to the heavens under the influence of drumming, hallucinatory materials, isolation, and deprivation. Anthropologists have documented a number of stages in this three-day flight cycle (Eliade 2004). A good case can be made that most of the petroglyph images depict various stages of the trance flight cycle as experienced by the shaman (Adams 2002). In my opinion the shaman or assistants to the shaman were the artists who made most of the images.

The Greaser Petroglyph Site was listed on the National Register of Historic Places in 1974. It is an easily reachable site consisting of a single boulder, located one half mile north of Oregon Highway 140, about five miles east of the village of Adel on a good gravel road.

10. Stone Corral & Warner Lakes

Along the west side of the Hart Mountain fault block is a series of lakes and wetlands some sixty miles long and eight miles wide. To the west lies the Warner Mountain range. During the Pleistocene Era the lakes were joined together in a single lake. In roughly the middle of the string of lakes, the Warner valley narrows. This narrow part of the valley is interesting both for its prehistory and recent history. Today's shallow lakes and wetlands support a variety of birds including migratory birds on the Pacific Flyway. (I remember visiting the Warner Valley as a youngster before most of the wetlands were drained for farming and marveling at the vast flocks of geese and ducks that rose in swarms from the wetlands in the fall and winter. Today some of the wetlands have been restored.) The chain of lakes today covers an area of 90,000 acres including 52,000 acres designated the Warner Wetlands Area of Critical Environmental Concern by the BLM.

The lakes in the Warner Valley have interesting names. From south to north are lakes Pelican, Crump, Hart, Anderson, Swamp,

Warner lakes

Stone corral at Stone Corral Lake

Mugwump, Flagstaff, Upper Campbell, Lower Campbell, Stone Corral, Turpin, and Bluejoint. Some—like Crump, Campbell, Hart, and Anderson—are named after pioneers, homesteaders, and early ranchers. Several—like Pelican and Swamp—are related to nature, and Bluejoint is named after a grass common in the area. Mugwumps were disaffected Republicans who bolted the party and supported the Democrats during the election of President Grover Cleveland in 1884.

Stone Corral Lake is named for the corral built on the shore of the lake by early ranchers, who probably hired Chinese labor to do the actual work. Warner Valley, Fort Warner, and the Warner Mountains were named for Captain William Warner, a West Point graduate who was given orders in 1849 to seek a railroad route from the headwaters of the Sacramento River to the Humbolt River across the Sierra Nevadas. Warner became lost and he and his party met many half-starved forty-niners who had split from the Applegate Trail at Goose Lake to go south to the goldfields instead of west into the valleys of Oregon. Somewhere near the current California-Oregon border, Warner and his party were attacked by hostile Indians. Warner and one of his men were killed, and Warner's body was never recovered.

The Warner Valley has no outlet to the sea, so the lakes fluctuate depending on the amount of water brought in by Deep Creek, Honey

Creek, and Twentymile Creek, and on the amount of evaporation which is in turn climate dependent. Crump Lake is 123 feet higher than Bluejoint Lake so the valley slopes to the north.

As a young Boy Scout, I spent many fine camping trips on Deep Creek and on Honey Creek in pursuit of redband trout. A hike up the Deep Creek canyon to the west of Highway 140 is an excellent way to see a typical desert canyon complete with aspen groves.

Despite the fact that the Warner Valley has been extensively drained for farming, its wetlands and lakes still provide significant habitat for birds. There are 239 species of birds that nest in and around the lakes including sandhill cranes, white pelicans, cormorants, herons, egrets, ibis, avocets, teal, swans, blackbirds, willets, phalaropes, and a variety of ducks. Finches, grosbeaks, woodpeckers, towhees, warblers, chickadees, bluebirds, owls, falcons, hawks, and golden and bald eagles also inhabit the riparian areas. Forty-two mammal species live near the Warner Lakes including pronghorn antelope, bighorn sheep, mule deer, elk, cougar, bobcat, and coyotes, as well as smaller animals such as jackrabbits, muskrats, squirrels, and chipmunks.

A visit to the Warner Valley requires a split trip. A paved road from the town of Plush crosses the lake chain just north of Hart Lake by the restored wetlands and a rest stop. Proceeding north to where the good road pitches up the slopes by Hart Mountain headquarters, the visitor can drive along the western foot of the Hart Mountain block with the lakes to the west. This road, which leads to Stone Corral, is very muddy and impassable during the spring runoff and is best tackled later in the summer. The sunstone collection area is located to the north of Plush on a different road.

Going south from the rest stop at Hart Lake along the west side of Hart Mountain with the lakes to the right (west), the traveler will come to Stone Bridge—a significant petroglyph site as well as an interesting site in the military history of the region (see Chapter 11). Proceeding south from Stone Bridge the traveler will pass hot springs and another stone corral while eventually arriving at Greaser Petroglyph. Just beyond Greaser Petroglyph to the south is Highway 140 with the town of Adel visible to the west.

11. Stone Bridge & Camp Warner

STONE BRIDGE IS LOCATED between Hart Lake and Crump Lake where the Warner Valley narrows. The story of Stone Bridge begins with the U.S. Army's campaign to subdue Northern Paiute bands in northern California and southeastern Oregon. Old Camp Warner was used as winter headquarters in 1866–1867. A unit was sent from Fort Boise along the east side of the Warner Valley to locate a fort but they were unable to cross the chain of lakes and wetlands, so the camp was established on the eastern slope of Hart Mountain. It was a hard winter at the high elevation, and one sergeant froze to death. General George Crook ordered the camp moved to the Honey Creek area of the Warner Mountains site west of the Warner Lakes, where it was renamed Fort Warner. To get the wagons and equipment across the narrows between Hart Lake and Crump Lake, a detachment of forty men built a bridge made of basalt boulders and rocks across the marshy area during the summer months of 1867. The bridge was built at the foot of a major petroglyph field on boulders near the lake. Some of the smaller boulders used to construct the bridge may have had petroglyphs. The petroglyph field is not mentioned in the autobiography of General Crook (Crook 1960).

Pictographs painted on a rock at the Stone Bridge site

Fort Warner (also known as New Camp Warner) was lower in elevation and enjoyed a less severe winter climate, although the fort was still isolated during winter storms. The new site was forested, so the military brought in a sawmill to construct regular barracks and buildings. Several women, including Mrs. Crook, called the fort home. One of the officer's wives, Julia Gillis, left a vivid, firsthand account of life at Fort Warner. "Many of the officers and ladies are preparing for an excursion down to Goose Lake," she wrote, "but the distance is so great they will be three or four days and the roads are only passable by saddle animals so I am not going as I cannot take the Baby" (Gillis 1993).

About 280 troops were stationed at the fort under General Crook, who used the fort to support cavalry, mounted infantry, and Indian scouts in Snake War campaigns against the Northern Paiute bands. The war ended in 1869 with a treaty signed by the Paiute chief Wewawewa. The fort was abandoned in 1874. Little physical evidence remains of either Old or New Camp Warner.

After New Camp Warner was abandoned, Stone Bridge was still used on the route of the Oregon Central Military Road. The road was originally intended to be a route between Fort Boise and Eugene, Oregon. Large land grants were given to support the road but it never was much of a road. In reality the military road was more of a fraudulent land grab. The road bisected the Klamath Indian reservation, and in a 1908 decision by Justice Oliver Wendell Holmes, the U.S. Supreme Court sided with the road company claiming ownership of the land. In 1938, the Klamath tribe took the case back to the Supreme Court and won a settlement of $5.3 million (Minor et al. 1979). In 1974 the bridge and the road were placed on the National Register of Historic Places.

12. Sunstone Collection Site

Rock and mineral collectors should not pass up an opportunity to search for the state's official gemstone—the Oregon sunstone. The sunstone is a type of feldspar found in Norway, eastern Oregon, and several other places in the United States. The Oregon sunstone has inclusions of copper that give it a shimmering optical effect known as "shiller" or "aventurescence." Shiller is caused by light reflecting from minute parallel metallic plates found in the sunstone. When viewed at right angles to the plates, light is reflected to the eye. Red sunstone contains the highest percentage of copper at up to 200 parts per million (Geitgey 1987). Sunstone is translucent to transparent and can be found in clear, yellow, red, green, and blue varieties. The most common are pale yellow; red and other colors are considered more valuable.

Oregon sunstones are a calcium-rich variety of plagioclase feldspar named labradorite, a common mineral in basaltic lava flows. Sunstone occurs in basalt flows exposed by weathering—in this region from Steens Mountain volcanoes that erupted thirteen to fourteen million years ago into a vast lake. The basalt flow was underwater for thousands of years before being exposed by a drying lake and weathering.

There are three sunstone locations in Oregon. The Lake County site is largest at about seven square miles; the two Harney County locations are less than a square mile each. The Oregon Sunstone Public Collection Area in Lake County between the Warner Valley and Abert Rim, twenty-three miles north of Plush, provides the public an opportunity to collect sunstones. A brochure with a good map is available from the BLM office in Lakeview, or online at www.blm.gov/or/districts/lakeview. The Plush store offers water, groceries, gasoline, and a selection of cut sunstones for sale.

13. Petroglyph Lake

As Petroglyph Lake dries in the spring and summer, distinct bands of vegetation rim the lake, lending intense color to the scene. The plant community around the lake includes currant, big sagebrush, arrowleaf balsamroot, great basin wildrye, and biscuitroot.

Petroglyph Lake is located on the Hart Mountain National Antelope Refuge, which was established in 1936 to provide range for the rapidly dwindling populations of pronghorn antelope throughout the West. The refuge consists of 278,000 acres and is home to some three hundred species of wildlife including California bighorn sheep, mule deer, sage grouse, and redband trout.

Though not on the scale of Long Lake, Petroglyph Lake is one of the Oregon high desert's significant petroglyph sites. Current thinking attributes the lake's petroglyphs, lithic scatters, rock cairns, and rock circles to ancestors of the Modoc and Klamath cultures. The cairns

Petroglyph Lake and yellow rabbitbrush

and circles are also known as prayer seats. The prayer seats (Daehnke and Raymond 2008) and petroglyphs are artifacts associated with shamanic trance flights or vision quests. At the lake there are some sixty-five petroglyph panels with about 360 individual designs. The designs range from animal figures that appear to be antelope and bighorn sheep to lizards; human and animal morphs; anthropomorphic animal forms; stretched man figures (resembling the sculptures of Giacometti); shaman figures in leaping postures; abstract figures including circle portals, some concentric (entry points to the underworld), and lines of power (dot lines representing the flight path of the shamans); dumbbell figures; and wave lines.

Petroglyph Lake is accessible from the main road leading to Hart Mountain Refuge headquarters from the west. High clearance is recommended since the road is rock strewn and deeply rutted in places. Two unnamed lakes to the north of Petroglyph Lake make for a nice side hike.

14. Lake Abert ❦ Chandler State Park

I HAVE NEVER BEEN TO LAKE ABERT when the wind was not blowing. When I drive along Highway 395 south along the eastern shore of the lake, I stop at turnouts periodically to view birds on the lake to the west, to search for petroglyphs on the lichen covered boulders, or to scan the faulted rim to the east for bighorn sheep. I am always absorbed in the stunning beauty and primordial nature of this place, where geology, biology, and history come to the surface in stark relief.

Abert Rim and Lake Abert exemplify horst and graben geology (blocks pushed upwards by faults alternating with blocks that have dropped). East of the lake the Abert Rim fault block extends some 2,000 feet above the lake, looming over the scene like a long basalt wall. To the west a tilted basin sixteen miles long and six miles wide holds in the saline waters of the lake. Because the lake has no outlet, accumulated brine has made Lake Abert a saline inland sea. During the waning of the last ice age in the Pleistocene era, Lake Abert was part of a much larger lake covering much of south-central Oregon,

Lake Abert horst and graben fault block

Lake Chewaucan. Today the Chewaucan River runs into the lake from the forested regions west of Paisley, Oregon. Chewaucan is a Native American word meaning "place of roots or bulbs." Today the ancient shorelines of Lake Chewaucan can still be seen, etched on the rim rocks throughout southeastern Oregon, including Fort Rock many miles to the west of Lake Abert.

Because its salinity is higher than that of the sea, Lake Abert is host to salt-tolerant organisms such as *Artemia salina*, or brine shrimp (Phillips and Van Denburgh 1985). The brine shrimp and brine flies are a rich source of protein, making Lake Abert an important stop for birds, especially shore birds, migrating on the Pacific Flyway. I have observed brine flies on the shores of the lake so thick that they created dense, black, ankle-deep clouds along the ground, and thousands of phalaropes twirling in the water to stir up brine shrimp. A significant portion of the western snowy plover, eared grebes, American avocets, and Wilson's and red-necked phalaropes on the Pacific Flyway use Lake Abert on their migratory travels. In addition, raptors and migratory ducks and geese frequent the lake. The sage, rabbitbrush, crested wheatgrass, juniper, and native bunch grass around the lake support a variety of large mammals including mule deer, California bighorn sheep, pronghorn antelope, coyotes, bobcats, and cougars. Some fourteen animal species at Lake Abert are assigned special status by the State of Oregon or the federal government.

Whenever I visit Lake Abert, I am compelled to photograph the lichens growing on the basalt boulders at the foot of Abert Rim. The bright red and orange lichens thrive in the intense high-altitude sun exposed to the incessant southwest winds. These symbiotic combinations of fungus and algae manage to grow for decades in the harsh conditions while eventually breaking down the rocks they live on to form soils—hence their status as "pioneer" plants. As long as they are there, I know the air at Lake Abert is clean and pure because the lichens are sensitive to air pollution.

One of the first Europeans to see Lake Abert was fur trader Peter Skene Ogden. Later John Work of the Hudson's Bay Company travelled the west side of the lake looking for beaver. However, the lake was named by explorer John C. Fremont in honor of his superior, Col. John James Abert, the head of the Corps of Topographical Engineers. In his journal, Fremont called Lake Abert "a handsome sheet of water" and "this forbidding lake" (Fremont 1845).

When archaeologist Richard Pettigrew undertook a survey for the state highway department along thirteen miles of the east shore of Lake Abert (the route of Highway 395) he exclaimed in his report, "As I clambered over the rocks, finding yet another such site around each bend, my normal restraint slipped away and I found myself shouting and gasping with incredulity." He was referring to some 441 circular stone features indicating the presence of dwellings or structures as well as petroglyphs and concentrations of lithic tools (Pettigrew 1985). There is strong evidence that permanent villages existed on the shores of Lake Abert for extended periods since the last ice age. The stone circles were perhaps covered with brush or mats to form conical roofs. Clues to the age of the Chewaucan Culture are found to the west at Fort Rock on the larger pluvial Lake Chewaucan, which once included present day Lake Abert. At caves near Fort Rock, the father of Oregon archaeology, Dr. Luther Cressman, found sagebrush sandals dating back some 9,000 years. The earliest known occupation of the area was 13,200 years ago according to Cressman. (More recent studies at nearby Paisley Caves have dated occupation back to 14,000 or more years before present.) Perhaps the Chewaucan culture was related to the present day Klamath tribe located currently to the west of Lake Abert.

A number of walls of stacked basalt rock extend upslope from near the shores of the lake toward the sheer basalt rim rock towering over the lake to the east. Some of these rock walls may have been built by the Chewaucan people, but others were no doubt built by pioneer stockmen who may have used contracted Chinese labor.

On Highway 395 south of Lake Abert is a small park named after a pioneer rancher in the area. Chandler State Park features a small, mature stand of ponderosa pine, a marsh, and a stream—Crooked Creek—for fishing. This childhood haunt of mine is a peaceful place to stop while travelling to or from Lake Abert.

15. Alkali Lake & the Hutton Tui Chub

ALKALI LAKE IS A PLAYA LAKE (a drying lake with no outlet) north of Lake Abert. During Pleistocene times the lake was 270 feet deep. The basin floor is covered by beds of clay, silt, volcanic ash, pumice, and deposits of alluvium and soda. The shorelines from the ancient lakes are clearly visible on the rims to the south of the lake. The brine water can be as high as pH 11 with the silica content up to 2,500 ppm. Today the dry lake is surrounded by a greasewood flat.

Near the west side of the lake is Hutton Spring, the only habitat for the Hutton tui chub, a unique species listed as threatened in 1985. Hutton Spring has varied from twenty to forty feet across and up to fifteen feet deep in the center, and is surrounded by sedge, tules, and saltgrass. Hutton Spring was once a stagecoach stop, but today it is a fenced, isolated spring surrounded by alkali flats.

Alkali Lake is remarkable for the formation of Magadiite—a precipitate of pothole brine. Part of the playa is covered by circular depressions or potholes in the wet, green mud that are filled with crystalline sodium salts (natron and trona). Magadiite occurs in the mud in veins four to fifteen inches wide and about an inch high, made of a hard, crumbly, porcelain-like substance. The veins form a pattern of rectangles that stretches across the playa.

During World War II, Alkali Lake was part of a United States Army training exercise called the Oregon Maneuver. In 1943 some 100,000 soldiers participated in training across 10,000 square miles and seven counties of central Oregon. Temperature extremes of fifty degrees in twenty-four hours, dust storms, vast distances, and desert terrain tested the troops. The airfield at Alkali Lake today is an improved strip known as the Alkali Lake State Airport—an emergency field. I remember as a young lad in Lakeview seeing long trains with flatcars loaded with tanks and trucks parked near town with hundreds of soldiers attending them. The troops trained in the desert country, including

Alkali Lake, later served in North Africa, the Philippines, Okinawa, France, Italy, and Germany.

Years later, Alkali Lake became infamous in relation to another war. In 1969 an Oregon company was given a permit to dispose of 25,000 fifty-gallon drums of chemical waste associated with the production of Agent Orange during the Vietnam War. The chemicals included dioxins and phenols. In 1976 the rusting drums were crushed in trenches and covered with soil and gravel. Groundwater around the pits has been contaminated. Despite legal action the State of Oregon has recovered from the chemical company only a small portion of the cost of monitoring the site. Now surrounded by fence, the isolated site has not been cleaned up, and may never be. Despite wars and toxic waste, the tiny Hutton tui chub clings to survival as it has for thousands of years—a remnant of the past in a small spring in a vast desert.

16. Willow Ranch ❦ Goose Lake

THE STORY OF WILLOW RANCH reflects the history of the West as a whole, from Native American occupation to early exploration, pioneer settlement, ranching and farming, a resort era and land rush, a gold rush, timber harvesting, and sawmilling.

Willow Ranch is set in spectacular terrain, at 4,700 feet in elevation, nine miles south of the Oregon border in Modoc County. To the east rise the Warner Mountains—a fault-block range sixty-five miles long running north and south from California into Oregon. To the immediate west of the ranch is shallow Goose Lake, some twenty-five miles long and four to six miles wide, with no drainage to the sea. Highway 395 is nearby, as is Goose Lake 55 Railroad, a rail line connecting the fifty-five miles from Alturas, California, to Lakeview, Oregon (Myrick 1962).

Today the field at Willow Ranch is overgrown with weeds and rabbitbrush amid patches of dry, cracked ground. Crumbling concrete foundations arise from the brush, and here and there are piles of rusting metal plates, forged tools, vessels, and cables. Incongruous valves and pipes spring up from the ground, connected to some long buried underworld network. A few large artifacts remain including a hundred-foot-tall wigwam wood waste burner, a large metal cyclone, and two boats once used to push log rafts across Goose Lake. The weed-filled depression of what was once a millpond today stands as a dry anachronism. A commemorative sign surrounded by a link chain and mounted on a mill wheel tells the brief history of a once-flourishing example of the lumber and sawmill era. Cattle graze on the site in blatant disrespect for the artifacts of the mill culture that contributed materials for the building of the West.

The first group to inhabit the area was the Hewisedawi group of the Achomawi tribe—known today as the Pit River tribe. Fred Kniffen in his work on the Achomawi identified two settlements on the east shore of Goose Lake near the current location of Willow Ranch (Kniffen

Willow Ranch wood waste "wigwam" burner

1928). The Pit River tribe was known for building pits to trap deer and game. Today only arrowheads, obsidian scatters, and petroglyphs testify to Achomawi occupation of the area.

17. Lily Lake & High Grade Mines

LILY LAKE IS A SMALL, picturesque, high-mountain lake close to the Oregon border in the Modoc National Forest in California. It is an excellent place to fly fish for feisty trout. Lily Lake and nearby Cave Lake occupy a cirque made by a small glacier in the Pleistocene era. Both lakes are dammed by moraine deposited by the glacier (Hill 1915) and both are located on a foundation of rhyolite—an extrusive volcanic rock. The Pine Creek canyon leading up to Lily Lake is heavily forested and steep.

Lily Lake, true to its name, is home to a healthy community of water lilies. The flat leaves of the water lily are waxy and water-repellent on the top. They float because of surface tension on the underside of the leaves. A hollow leaf stem helps the lily float, and transports air to the underwater rhizomes.

When the water is calm and reflections abound, the lake looks like a painting by Monet. Quaking aspen provide a nice backdrop to the scene and sometimes an eagle can be seen patrolling the lake. One spring on the steep road up to Lily Lake, I saw a small pond near the road covered with dragonflies. The dragonflies were prolific and were mating. It was quite a sight to behold.

Gold was discovered near Lily Lake in the 1860s. The U.S. Army in 1865 established Fort Bidwell at the eastern base of the Warner Mountains intending to pacify local Paiute tribes. That year a rancher named Daniel Hoag was hired by the army as a guide. Speculation abounded that Hoag had discovered a gold bonanza in the Warner Mountains but Hoag took his secret with him when he was killed two years later in an Indian battle. He is nevertheless credited with the discovery of the High Grade Mining District (Palmer 1991). A renewed frenzy for gold began in 1905, and the arrival of the Nevada-California-Oregon Railway in 1912 allowed ore to be freighted down from the mines to a rail stop at the town of New Pine Creek. The mining era gave rise to such colorful legends as that of High Grade Annie, who drove ore wagons down the steep road to the railhead. A total of seventy-one claims were filed, some of which were worked via tunnels and shafts. At the Mountain View mine, a stamp mill, cyanide plant, and an aerial tramway operated until World War I.

The names of the claims themselves tell stories. Some names derive from the history of gold mining: Big Bonanza, Bonanza King, Comstock, Klondike, Alaska Bell, and Yukon. Some are simply hopeful like Happy Thought and Dandy, while others like Bad Bill, Printer Boy, and Uncle Joe suggest a specific person. Some are named after natural features: Emerald, Diamond Fraction, Gold Peak, Huckleberry, Pink Rose, Red Quartz, Spearmint, Sugar Pine, White Quartz, Topaz, Red Horse, Sea Lion, and Tamarack. Even the cycle of the day is covered with Sunrise and Sunset.

By the spring of 1912 the town of High Grade was established, with two post offices, several restaurants, hotels, a bakery, and of course, an assay office. Telephone lines linked the town with New Pine Creek to the west and Fort Bidwell to the east (Palmer 1991). The site was virtually inaccessible during the winter and the name High Grade seems to refer more to the steep road to the town rather than the quality of the ore. Despite all the hype, it is unlikely that the High Grade District ever produced more than $100,000 in gold during its entire existence.

The visitor today can see remains of the wooden and log structures from the heyday of activity at the High Grade mines. Formidable rock piles at the site are not the result of mining activity but are angular talus blocks up to six feet across. The talus in some places is twenty feet thick. The piles are the result of differential weathering and frost wedging of rhyolite. The rock piles were an obstacle to some of the mining activities.

High Grade and Lily Lake are accessible by a steep gravel road from Highway 395 near New Pine Creek. Combining this trip with a visit to Willow Ranch offers a good introduction to the natural and human history of the Warner Mountain range.

18. Dog Lake

When I was growing up in Lakeview, Dog Lake was one of my favorite places to go fishing. Although not a desert lake like those to the east, the lake was high (5,197 feet) and in the Goose Lake drainage basin. At that time the lake was a private holding within the boundaries of Fremont National Forest. My father and I would rent a boat to go after the large bass in the lake. Now owned by the federal government, Dog Lake features two Forest Service campgrounds and a boat launch. It is still an excellent fishing spot for rainbow trout, bass, crappie, perch, and catfish.

The Nature Conservancy—which helped get Dog Lake into public ownership—has described the lake as a rare example of a medium-sized, montane, freshwater lake in near natural condition. The lake features both floating and rooted macrophytes (aquatic plants), and marshes lining the lakeshore provide good habitat for waterfowl, including a variety of ducks and coots. Meadows surrounding the lake incline to stands of ponderosa pine and juniper forest.

The lake's depth varies from an average of thirteen feet to a maximum of twenty feet (Johnson 1998). It is deeper than other lakes in the area, which makes it less alkaline. However, because of the macrophytes, the lake bottom is devoid of dissolved oxygen. The water is transparent with some *Microcystis* and *Anabaena* algae blooms.

Dog Lake is home to the curious blind catfish (*Ictalurus nebulosus*), also known as the brown bullhead. "In a recent catch of fourteen, I found only one with normal eyes; seven with no external evidence of eyes, and six with left eyes only. Apparently sight is not an evolutionary advantage in the boggy parts of the lake or under the overhanging banks where these fish live" (Weisel 1964).

In 1934 Dog Lake was the site of a Civilian Conservation Corp (CCC) camp. It was a summer camp and its main purpose was to fight forest fires. Once a busy settlement with tents, a mess hall, bathhouse, latrine, bakery, and electric light-shed, no trace of the camp remains.

19. Chewaucan River

THE CHEWAUCAN RIVER originates from springs on heavily forested Gearhart Mountain. The forests in the upper river watershed consist of ponderosa pine including some old growth groves, lodgepole pine, and white fir. Water from Antelope Springs and Ben Young, Coffeepot, Corral, Dog, Sage Hen, Bear, and Mill Creeks join the river before it flows through the town of Paisley, Oregon. The river flows into the Upper and Lower Chewaucan marsh and then into Lake Abert, which has no drainage.

Chewaucan is a Klamath Indian word meaning "wild potato place." Tribes dug for roots and tubers in the marsh land in the lower Chewaucan drainage. The original marsh was covered with tufted hairgrass, redtop, sedges, and rushes. Today the marshland is controlled by a system of weirs and irrigation canals so that it can be used for pasture. The land around the marsh is highly alkaline soil that supports salt tolerant plants.

As a young Boy Scout, I camped on the Chewaucan River and fished for native redband trout. At that time, the river also was home to planted eastern brook and rainbow trout as well as German brown trout. The Oregon Department of Fish and Wildlife stopped stocking the river in 1998 in an effort to restore native redband populations. In its natural state, the redband grew to thirty inches in the marsh, where it could feast on abundant insect life, most notably mosquitoes. Genetic testing showed that the native trout had not interbred with the stocked fish and after stocking was stopped, the native population rebounded. However, man-made obstacles like weirs prevented the fish from returning to the headwaters of the river to spawn. Various agencies worked to reopen the river to fish by replacing old culverts and the Paisley town weir. These and other projects have led to the return of large native redband trout in the upper river. The town of Paisley, Oregon, holds both an annual fishing derby to celebrate the return of the trout, and a mosquito festival.

The upriver region has also been the object of restoration efforts including fencing of riparian areas from grazing, placing wood debris and boulder clusters in the river for fish cover, and removal of juniper from stretches of the watershed to increase water flow.

The river and marshes also support habitat for migrating waterfowl like snow geese, cormorants, and herons. Sandhill cranes, ibis, egrets, and a variety of ducks also nest on the river.

The river and canyon are quite spectacular, particularly in the fall. There are several campgrounds to choose from in the Paisley area. The road up the river is good and paved part way. One of my summer jobs in the Forest Service was to survey this road.

20. Gearhart Mountain

Gearhart Mountain in the Fremont National Forest is the site of the only casualties suffered on U.S. soil as a result of enemy action during World War II (Mikesh 1978). In May of 1945, a Japanese balloon bomb killed five children and one adult who were on a picnic on the mountain. A monument at the Mitchell Recreation Area marks the spot of the tragedy.

The mountain was named for two brothers who were ranchers in the area in the 1870s. Gearhart Mountain was designated a Wilderness Area in 1964 with additional lands added in 1984, bringing the total to 22,800 acres.

Gearhart Mountain is a high peak of 8,364 feet and is located between two physiographic provinces—the Cascade Mountains, and Basin and Range (Larson 2007). Geologically the mountain is a shield volcano made of low silica, low viscosity lava flows. Of the four types of volcanoes, shield volcanoes have the gentlest slopes (less than 8 degrees) and can be up to 100 miles in diameter (Lillie 2005). Composite volcanoes such as Mount Mazama (Crater Lake), Mount Rainier, and Mount Shasta have slopes of ten to twenty degrees and are one to ten miles in diameter. These are formed of high silica, higher viscosity lava. A lava dome is much smaller than a composite volcano but has slopes of at least twenty degrees. Cinder cones such as those found at Diamond Craters have slopes of thirty degrees and are less than a mile in diameter, and are low silica composition.

At Gearhart Mountain differential erosion has weathered porphyritic rocks into fascinating shapes called the Palisades, Lookout Rock, the Dome, and Haystack Rock. Some of the rocks resemble large beehives. Among the Palisade rocks, stunted ponderosa pines grow from cracks and pockets of soil.

Like Steens Mountain and parts of the Warner Mountains, Gearhart Mountain was glaciated during the Pleistocene. Cirques, like the two-mile-wide Dairy Creek cirque, were formed on the north and west side of the mountain. Dairy Creek feeds the Chewaucan River, which in turn drains into Lake Abert in the Great Basin. Talus slopes and slide debris line the steep headwalls of the cirque. Blue Lake occupies one of the cirques on the mountain and is blocked by a moraine.

Wildlife on Gearhart Mountain includes bears and mountain lions. There are 250 plant species identified on the mountain. The meadows, ponds, and wetlands in the cirques contain a variety of wildflowers, grasses, and aspen groves. On the lower slopes are ponderosa pine, whitebark pine, and lodgepole pine, while the higher slopes feature pure stands of lodgepole pine and whitebark pine. Stands of old growth forest persist on the mountain thanks to its designation as a protected wilderness area.

It is unlikely that the high meadows have ever been grazed, and an amazing collection of wildflowers peak there in July. Several endemics are listed on Oregon Natural Heritage Program lists, including blue-leaved penstemon, green-tinged paintbrush (also found at Lost Forest), and discoid goldenweed (Larson 2007).

While much of the timberland outside of the wilderness area has been logged, Gearhart Mountain remains beautiful. When I surveyed logging roads in the area during the summers while working my way through college, I loved sitting under a ponderosa pine for lunch and soaking in the high mountain air, and the scent of the trees, and the sounds of the breezes. I always wondered if those groves would survive the power saw and some of them have.

21. Sycan Marsh

SYCAN MARSH is a fifty square-mile wetland fed by the Sycan River. The headwaters of the Sycan River are located in the Fremont National Forest. The upper fifty-nine miles of the river are designated in the National Wild and Scenic Rivers System. Sycan is derived from the Klamath term "saiga keni," meaning level, grassy place.

Sycan Marsh is located about equidistant between Silver Lake to the north and Bly to the south. The land is owned by the Nature Conservancy with the ZX Ranch holding a grazing lease. Migrating and nesting birds use the wetlands, which are also home to threatened fish including bull trout and redband trout. Thousands of tundra swans stop at the marsh on their northward migration. Breeding sandhill cranes, black terns, white-faced ibis, and yellow rails also inhabit the marsh, along with forty other species of waterfowl and water birds, including white pelicans, Forster's terns, and white-fronted geese. Ducks breeding at the preserve include the cinnamon teal, blue-winged teal, northern shoveler, redhead, canvasback, ring-necked duck, common merganser, wood duck, and mallard. Raptor residents include bald eagles, red-tailed hawks, and goshawks.

New species of mollusks—mussels, lamprey, snails, and other aquatic organisms—have been discovered in Sycan marsh. The wetland includes a variety of grasses from wooly sedge and marsh buttercup to common camas, once a food staple for Native Americans.

During the twentieth century the marsh was drained for grazing to the detriment of wildlife. The Nature Conservancy and ZX Ranch are collaborating on research designed to demonstrate how good ranching practices can be compatible with wetland restoration. Research includes radio telemetry studies of bull and redband trout, a botanical study of a highly unusual groundwater-fed fen, and breeding surveys of the elusive yellow rail. (A fen is a marshland that has neutral or alkaline water chemistry and relatively large quantities of dissolved minerals, but few other plant nutrients.)

The Sycan Marsh is a great example of what good science and restoration practices can do to rebuild an important ecosystem.

Cottonwood Meadows

22. Cottonwood Meadows

When I worked for the Forest Service during summers of my college years, I surveyed a site for a dam at Cottonwood Meadows, just south of Cougar Peak between Quartz Mountain and Five Corners. In 1961 the Forest Service build a small earthen dam on Cottonwood Creek to create a small lake. Today, Cottonwood Lake is a eutrophic lake with high phosphorus concentrations, high pH, and low water transparency. It has natural algal blooms (*Anabaena* and *Gloeotrichia*) and macrophytes cover a large portion of the lake, particularly in late summer. The lake will eventually revert to its original meadow form.

Cottonwood Lake is one of my favorite places in the Oregon Outback. Old growth ponderosa pines tower nearby, and at the northern shore of the lake are fine examples of quaking aspen groves. Ducks and beaver ply the waters while raptors circle overhead on fishing expeditions. I have also witnessed remarkable swarms of dragonflies at the lake.

One of Cottonwood's most interesting natural features is a remarkable meadow of yellow skunk cabbage (*Lysichiton americanus*) on the wet ground just west of the lake. The large, tropical-looking swamp plant has brilliant yellow spathes (Clark 1998). To me, the plant does not really smell like the spray of a skunk. Bears consume the whole plant and certainly bears have been reported at Cottonwood Meadows.

When the late 1950s uranium craze settled over Oregon's remote corner, drug stores sold Geiger counters for weekend prospectors. During that time many claims were filed near Cottonwood Meadow and many other places in the Fremont Forest. Fortunately these claims were never mined.

Cottonwood Lake features two campgrounds and a boat ramp, and the lake is stocked with rainbow and brook trout. No motor boats are allowed on the lake, but it is a perfect place to canoe.

23. Summer Lake Hot Springs and Summer Lake Refuge

SUMMER LAKE HOT SPRINGS, near the town of Paisley, is a 145-acre resort featuring geothermal springs averaging 113° F. Legend has it that cowboys used to bathe at the springs in a canoe filled with hot spring water, and a canoe is still present at the site today. In 1928, a wooden and metal shed was built to cover a thirty-by-fifty-foot concrete pool. This shed still stands over the pool, and there are several outdoor rock pools on the grounds.

When I was a youngster in the mid-1940s, my parents and I would take a trip to the hot springs to visit my grandmother who lived in a small house on the property. The house stands today as a rental cabin. I loved swimming in the pool, where the water made my skin feel soft and silky like it was covered in talcum powder. My initials are still carved in the wood wall on the west side of the pool along with those of hundreds of other bathers from over the years. Many believe these waters have curative powers.

Summer Lake Hot Springs pool

Winter Ridge

Summer Lake Hot Springs is at the foot of Winter Ridge, a fault block at the extreme northwest corner of the Great Basin. The ridge rises up to 3,100 feet from the basin floor. Large landslides have formed lake basins in the ridge. Summer Lake is a remnant of glacial Lake Chewaucan—a large Pleistocene lake that used to extend from current Summer Lake around to Lake Abert to the east. Pluvial Lake Chewaucan during the Pleistocene occupied 480 square miles and was up to 375 feet deep. Today the shores of the ancient lake can be seen on the foothills of Winter Ridge above the hot springs. On the heights above Winter Ridge to the west are stands of ponderosa pine while the Summer Lake basin is home to sagebrush and rabbitbrush. The more saline areas have greasewood, salt grass, and other halophytes. Sediments under pluvial Lake Chewaucan include oolites (egg stones), peat, diatomite, volcanic tuff, and a bed of compacted mollusk shells. Fossils found in the lake basin include camel, horse, bison, peccary, and swan.

In the Paisley Caves about five miles north of the hot springs, bones, human coprolites, and sagebrush twigs were found that dated to 14,000+ years BP, indicating pre-Clovis occupation (Maugh 2012).

To fully understand Summer Lake Hot Springs in the context of the history of the American West, it is necessary to consider one of its most important figures—John C. Fremont. Fremont was a complex and colorful man—military officer, senator, presidential candidate, explorer of the west, military governor of California, and wealthy businessman. On his expedition to the West in 1843-44, Fremont's party included legendary scout Kit Carson, two Delaware Indians, mountain man Thomas Fitzpatrick, a freed black man named Jacob Dodson, and a number of Metis and French Canadians. Near current Klamath Falls, Fremont saved Kit Carson's life in a battle with Indians. Travelling east from the Klamath basin, Fremont arrived at the top of a ridge overlooking a vast lake below. Fremont named the ridge Winter Ridge and the lake Summer Lake because the lake seemed remarkably summer-like compared to the rim, which was covered in December snow. Fremont also was the first to document Lake Abert, naming it after his superior Col. J. J. Abert, chief of the Corps of Topographic Engineers. Fremont was the first American to see Lake Tahoe, determined that the Great Basin was endorheic (lacking an outlet to the sea), and mapped volcanoes such as Mount St. Helens. Fremont's published report to Congress became an important guide for pioneers heading west. The forested parts of Winter Ridge became part of Fremont National Forest as designated by Theodore Roosevelt. Features named in Fremont's honor include cities, parks, counties, streets, schools, an island, a river, an infantry division, a library, and twenty-two species of plants.

Summer Lake Wildlife Area is an 18,940 acre expanse of range land, meadows, wetlands, marshes, and playa located at the north end of the Summer Lake basin. The wetlands of the refuge are fed by a series of springs emerging at the foot of Winter Ridge via Ana River. The water in Ana River is naturally maintained at a constant 52° F. A series of manmade dikes and channels maintain the wildlife habitat. A project to replace diversion structures and to build bird-nesting islands was undertaken by a joint effort of a number of federal, state, and county agencies, Oregon State University, irrigation districts, and Ducks Unlimited. The project revitalized thousands of acres of nesting habitat. The refuge is also financially supported by hunter license fees.

The refuge supports 40 mammal species including aquatic animals like beaver and muskrat, 280 bird species, 15 reptile and amphibian species, and 8 fish species. The refuge is an important rest stop on the Pacific Flyway for hundreds of thousands of birds during spring and fall migrations. The birds using the refuge include upland game birds, songbirds, shorebirds, waterfowl, and birds of prey. The refuge offers four primitive camping sites, historic ranch structures, and artifacts including a barn and early ranching implements and machinery.

Slide lake and pine

24. Slide Lakes

Along the east side of Winter Ridge before it curves to the north, a number of massive landslides have created a series of cirque-like bowls. The landslides, with names like Slide Mountain, the Punchbowl, and Big Flat, each cover several square miles and extend to the present shoreline of Summer Lake. The bedrock consists of volcanic flows, sedimentary rocks, and pyroclastics, much of which is obscured by the landslide deposits. There are hanging bowls at Foster Creek and Bennett Flat indicating a fault, and it is possible that shifts along the fault created earthquakes that initiated the landslides. The landslides may have formed in the late Pleistocene. Because the landslides extended out to the current lakeshore, a saturated landslide mass and liquefaction may have contributed to the slides (Badger and Watters 2002).

Two lakes created by the slides that are worth visiting are within the designated Slide Mountain Geologic Area on Fremont National Forest. A trailhead to the lakes can be reached from Highway 31 travelling west from Summer Lake Hot Springs, with a left turn at Forest Road 29 and then a left turn at the fork onto Forest Road 017. The road is switch-backed and steep in places. Along the way are stunning views of the entire Summer Lake basin, small mountain streams, and meadows on the slopes. In the fall it is possible to find ripe, tasty, wild plums along the route.

The lakes are quite beautiful and are among my favorite trout fishing spots. When I was a child, my father took me on a hike to find the lakes he had heard were full of very large trout. This was before a good access road and trailhead was built. We got lost in the steep and rugged terrain and spent many hours trying to find our pickup. I don't remember catching any of the legendary trout that day.

The lakes are a photographer's paradise because of the old ponderosa pine near the shore reflecting in the waters, the dead tree snags flooded by the water, and the floating logs with miniature gardens growing on them. The colors and textures of the scene are stunning.

25. Fort Rock

Fort Rock is a tuff ring that indeed resembles a fort. It stands out on the former lakebed of Fort Rock Lake. The ring is approximately 4,550 feet in diameter and reaches some 200 feet high above the lake floor. At the end of the Pleistocene, Fort Rock Lake was about 150 feet deep and covered nearly 900 square miles. Ancient wave erosion carved terraces on Fort Rock including one estimated to be 14,000 years old. One of the terraces is visible more than sixty feet above the lake floor.

The tuff ring was formed perhaps 50,000 to 100,000 years ago when basalt magma rose through wet mud on the lake bottom. A jet of steam blew hot lava and ash into the air. As the blobs of lava and the ash

Fort Rock, with lake terrace to the left

settled down around the vent, a ring of tuff was formed. In Fort Rock Cave, on a tuff ring near Fort Rock, archaeologist Luther S. Cressman discovered sagebrush sandals and human artifacts dated to 9,000 to 10,000 years ago. Along with seventy-five sandals, Cressman and his team found long-stemmed points, Cascade points, lanceolate points, abraders, choppers, awls, scrapers, drills, stone knives, and gravers (Cressman 1981). In the last few years, findings at Paisley Caves southeast of Fort Rock have pushed the date of human occupation back to the pre-Clovis era, 14,000 or more years ago (Maugh 2012).

It is hard to imagine that the now-dry lakebeds and volcanic terrain of the Oregon Outback was one of the earliest sites of human habitation in North America. But some 14,000 years ago, the lakes teamed with fish and waterfowl beyond imagination.

26. Lost Forest

The Lost Forest is an isolated and anomalous ponderosa pine forest located in the Christmas Lake basin. The Lost Forest Research Natural Area was created by the BLM to protect this ancient stand of trees. Christmas Lake was a large pluvial lake in the Pleistocene era that has completely dried up. There are no springs or surface water in the Lost Forest.

The southwestern part of the area is covered by large shifting sand dunes, creating a dune field that is one of the largest in Oregon, comparable in size to those on the coast. The dunes are made of lacustrine (lake) sediments, aeolian (wind) deposits, and alluvial (stream deposit) materials. The dune field was created when homesteaders in the region broke the sagebrush and grass groundcover, exposing the soils. By the 1920s and '30s the homesteaders were starved out due to lack of water. Today however, deep aquifer wells enable significant farming in the Christmas Valley basin. Some trees have been smothered and killed by the dunes, but overall the forest is not threatened. It is highly unusual to see old growth trees in the high desert, where there is much less rainfall than these trees usually require. Their survival depends on the area's unique soil properties. Permeable sandy soils underlain with a hard caliche layer of calcium carbonate several inches thick retain and accumulate water in the root zone of the trees. Pumice sand from the eruption of Mount Mazama (Crater Lake) appears in surface soils throughout the Lost Forest. As a result, what rainwater falls quickly seeps into the ground before it can evaporate and is held above the caliche layer.

Another anomalous pine forest is Colvin Timbers to the east of Abert Rim. The nearest continuous pine forest is forty miles away. The Lost Forest is a remnant of ancient forests that covered central Oregon thousands of years ago. It is also home to the largest known juniper trees in Oregon at a height of sixty-eight feet.

The Lost Forest hosts a variety of large mammals including cougars, small mammals, and birds such as the magpie and mountain bluebird. Thirteen species of bats inhabit the forest. Shrub species include big sagebrush, bitterbrush, and rabbitbrush. Smaller shrubs, perennial grasses, and flowering plants also can be found in the forest, including the rare green-tinged paintbrush.

No grazing has been allowed in the forest since 1968. Timber sales removed trees in 1949 and again in 1955. A portable mill operated in the area. During WWII the area was used for military exercises as part of the Oregon Maneuver. Some abandoned homestead houses and barns are pocked with bullet holes from machine gun fire. Today the major threat to the forest is off-road vehicles that come in from the nearby dunes.

To get to the Lost Forest, travel east from the town of Christmas Valley on the Wagontire-Christmas Valley road, turn left (north) on Fossil Lake Road, and then right (east) on Lost Forest Road. Side trips near Christmas Valley include the Christmas Valley Air Force Station, Fossil Lake, Fort Rock and Fort Rock Homestead Village Museum, Crack-in-the-Ground, Devil's Garden, and the Black Hills Botanical Area.

27. Glass Buttes

APPROXIMATELY SEVENTY MILES east of Bend, Oregon, just to the south of Highway 20, Glass Buttes has been a favorite place for rock hounds for decades and is noted for its wide variety of obsidian. About 6,000 acres in the area have been designated a Free Use Public Area by the BLM.

Glass Buttes is a basalt-rhyolite volcanic feature that erupted 5.5 million years ago. The area lies within the Brothers Fault Zone, which extends from the Harney Basin to the Newberry Caldera. Along with obsidian and rhyolite, rock hunters can find hematite, hornblende, quartz, and biotite at Glass Buttes. The mineral cinnabar was mined for mercury in the area in the 1960s.

Most obsidian is black but Glass Buttes boasts an amazing variety: mahogany, red, flame, midnight lace, jet black, pumpkin, brown, rainbow, gold sheen, silver sheen, green, lizard skin, and snowflake (Miller 2013). Obsidian is natural glass with no sizable mineral crystals within the glass matrix. Obsidian forms from silica rich viscous magma—magma so viscous that crystals cannot grow before the magma cools and stops the crystal development. The various colors of obsidian are the result of opaque impurities or microscopic crystals. For example, red or brown obsidian contains tiny inclusions of hematite or limonite, both iron oxides. Tiny crystals of magnetite, biotite, or hornblende produce jet-black colors. Feldspar inclusions may yield blue, green, purple, or bronze colors. Feldspar or mica crystals oriented along lines of flow may produce rainbow obsidian (Miller 2013). Sheen varieties are caused by tiny gas bubbles stretched flat along flow lines.

It is rare to find obsidian older than 20 million years because over time it changes slowly from a glass to a rock as the silica molecules rearrange into crystal patterns—a process known as devitrification. This process causes obsidian to lose its glassy texture (Miller 2013).

Because of its sharp edges and strength Native Americans used obsidian from almost every location in North America to make arrowheads, spears, awls, needles, and other tools. Glass Butte obsidian was highly desired and traded over long distances, and has been found as far away as the Southwest United States.

PART TWO
Natural History

Animals

28. Beaver

ONE OF THE FIRST EXPLORERS into the Oregon desert was John Work of the Hudson's Bay Company and he was looking for beaver. It is no surprise the Oregon is known as the Beaver State.

Beavers were famously hunted for their pelts, and their glands were used for making perfume and medicine. The beaver population of North America may have once been as high as sixty million, but now it is estimated at only about one-tenth that number.

Beavers build their lodges in ponds, so they must first build a dam to make a pond. They use their formidable incisors to fell trees, which they then pile together and fill with branches, weeds, and mud.

Beavers use their flat tails to slap the water and sound an alarm when danger approaches. Their webbed hind feet help them dive and swim, and they are able to remain underwater for up to fifteen minutes. Beavers are nocturnal and do not hibernate. They store vegetation in a pile in the pond for sustenance during the winter. Beavers eat quaking aspen, cottonwood, willow, sedges, pondweed, and water lilies.

A beaver pond will eventually fill with sediment and become new meadowland, where new aspen groves can become established.

One night when I was camped on Deep Creek with my father, a large beaver joined us at our campfire. He sat there for the longest time, apparently fascinated with us or with the fire. More than once while fly fishing on a small desert stream, I found myself face-to-face with a beaver sitting under the cut bank a short distance away. Oftentimes we found the largest trout in the ponds behind the dams the industrious beavers had built.

29. Bighorn Sheep

THE BIGHORN SHEEP was thought to have crossed into North America via the Bering land bridge from Siberia during the Pleistocene. At one time, their population may have been in excess of one or two million, but by 1900 only several thousand remained. Since then the population has been restored.

Oregon's first bighorn sheep relocation occurred in 1954 when twenty California bighorns from British Columbia were released at Hart Mountain Antelope Refuge. Since then other bighorn sheep have been imported, sometimes by helicopter. The population of sheep in Oregon is now estimated to be in excess of 3,500. (Except for a small population of Rocky Mountain sheep in the Wallowa Mountains, the sheep in Oregon are California bighorns.) Today hunting of sheep is carefully regulated.

The male sheep have large, curved horns that can weigh thirty pounds. The horns of females are smaller and less curved. Rams tend to an individual ewe and block other males that try to take the ewe. Females form a stable hierarchy led by older females.

In eastern Oregon the sheep inhabit high, rugged, rocky cliffs. They are remarkably agile on the slopes and can withstand punishing winter weather at high altitudes. Cougars, coyotes, and eagles are their primary predators. The sheep graze on grasses and shrubs and use natural salt licks.

In Oregon's remote corner, the best places to look for bighorn sheep are on the slopes of Abert Rim, the Coglan Buttes area, Steens Mountain, or Hart Mountain. The return of the sheep in eastern Oregon is a good example of effective restoration practices for endangered wildlife.

30. Borax Lake Chub Foskett Speckled Dace

ALTHOUGH THEY ARE CLASSIFIED as different species, the Borax Lake chub, Foskett Spring speckled dace, and the Hutton tui chub have one important thing in common. They are all refugees isolated in small habitats since the Pleistocene pluvial lakes receded. They have survived in springs, and, in the case of the Borax Lake chub, in a small geothermal lake for thousands of years.

The Borax Lake chub is a dwarf form of genus *Gila* found only in Borax Lake. The fish is typically only two inches in length. It is similar to the Alvord Chub but has a longer, wider, and deeper head with larger eyes. The Borax chub feeds both on the lake bottom and the surface on larvae, diatoms, copepods, and insects. It is the only fish in Borax Lake and it favors the lake's cooler outflows. The species is listed as threatened.

The Foskett speckled dace (*Rhinichthys osculus*), like the Hutton tui chub (*Gila bicolor*), lives in isolated springs near the margins of dry playa lakebeds. They are both listed as threatened. The Foskett speckled dace is distinguished by large eyes and a dorsal fin set well behind. The only known population of this dace is in Foskett Spring near the west side of Coleman Lake. The spring originates in a pool about sixteen feet across that then flows towards Coleman Lake in a narrow, shallow channel. The pool has a sandy bottom and is thick with aquatic plants. The fish take cover under overhanging banks, grass and grass roots, and algae.

An attempt to establish a second population in Dace Spring, south of Foskett Spring, failed. Later the BLM acquired the parcel of land between the two springs and the site was fenced to exclude livestock. Two spring-fed pools were created and in 2010, fifty fish were moved successfully from Foskett to Dace Springs (Scheerer 2011).

The Hutton tui chub, the Foskett speckled dace, and the Borax Lake chub are all tenacious little creatures clinging to existence in a dry and salty land. With a little help from humans, they may survive another few thousand years.

31. Coyote

As a youngster I often watched coyotes hunting and chasing rabbits. With their sorrowful, nocturnal howls, they seemed to be solitary creatures and lonely.

Coyotes are very fast and agile. They can reach speeds up to forty-three miles per hour and jump over thirteen feet. The coyote can hear at a higher frequency than dogs.

Coyotes can dig their own burrows but they often use the burrows of badgers or groundhogs. They mark their territory with urine. Coyotes have adapted to the encroachment of humans and they reproduce even in urban and suburban settings. In order to adapt to humans, the coyote seems to be more nocturnal and to howl less. In the wild, coyotes can live about ten years.

In Native American mythology the coyote is a trickster or a hero or both. An example is the coyote in the creation story of the Achomawi—a tribe known as the Pit River Indians, who lived around Goose Lake and the Pit River. As in so many creation stories, the earth was originally water. A cloud formed and became lumpy and Coyote was formed. A fog arose and became lumpy and Silver Fox was formed. Together they thought a canoe into existence and floated in it for many years until it became mossy. While Coyote was asleep, Silver Fox created trees and rocks from combings from his hair. When Coyote woke up he began to eat the cherries, plums, and crickets that Silver Fox had made, but Silver Fox did not tell Coyote that he was the creator. After landing they built a sweat lodge and, using sticks of service berry that were stuck into the ceiling, they made people, animals, fish, and birds. In this story Coyote is the lazy and passive partner in creation. This is not an atypical depiction of the character of Coyote.

32. Great Basin Rattlesnake

GROWING UP CAMPING AND HIKING in the Oregon desert I was constantly wary of rattlesnakes. My scout troop killed a few snakes, some of which were as long as four to five feet, but usually we let them escape. We had to be particularly cautious near the feet of rim rocks or near boulders where the snakes would sun on the rocks or seek shelter on cold or hot days. Rattlesnakes shed their skin several times a year and it was not unusual to find shed skins. These snakes are buff, yellow-brown, or olive-brown, with patterns on their backs that enable them to blend in with the desert floor.

Rattlesnakes like temperatures between 80 and 90° F, but the desert has extremes of temperatures of fifty or more degrees per day. Therefore snakes hibernate in the winter and aestivate (spend much of the time in a state of torpor) in the summer. They are fond of southern exposures, particularly after cold desert nights.

Author as a young man with rattlesnake

Rattlesnakes have heat-sensing pits in their heads enabling them to find prey at night. They can see color but their sight is not particularly acute. The snakes can also smell their prey with their tongues and small nostrils. They have no external ear openings but they can sense vibrations in the ground. Rattlesnakes warn potential predators by the use of rattles—hollow segments made of keratin that are vibrated by tremendously fast muscles. Rattlesnakes prey on small birds and small rodents. Their fangs inject a hemotoxin into the prey that kills tissue, and causes swelling and bleeding. The snakes in turn are prey for king snakes, hawks, eagles, and large animals like raccoons. Rattlesnakes are declining in many parts of the west because of loss of habitat and human predation. Some naturalists think that some snakes are evolving to avoid detection by no longer rattling.

33. Jackrabbit & Mountain Cottontail

THE BLACK-TAILED JACKRABBIT makes its home on the sage flats on the Oregon steppe. Historical photographs show huge piles of jackrabbits killed by homesteaders in Christmas Valley who conducted "rabbit drives" to reduce the staggering population of rabbits that decimated their crops.

Black-tailed jackrabbit

Jackrabbits are extremely fast, capable of clocking forty miles per hour, and able to leap ten feet. They run in fits and starts to evade predators like coyotes or hawks. They have enormously long ears that appear almost translucent when lit from behind. They build simple nests above ground and do not migrate or hibernate. They feed on sagebrush, greasewood and Russian thistle, among other plants.

In the spring the rabbits dance in a frenzy, leading to the saying "mad as a March hare." They also engage in a strange boxing display that is perhaps a breeding behavior.

Unlike the jackrabbit, which is basically inedible, the mountain cottontail was a food source for pioneers and is still eaten by modern day hunters. The cottontail is much smaller than the jackrabbit, with shorter ears and a white tail and underside and lives around big sagebrush, rabbitbrush, and saltbush. The cottontail is not a social animal and did not appear to have the kind of population explosions that made the jackrabbit become a major pest to farmers.

34. Mule Deer

THE MULE DEER was an important food supply in my youth. We hunted mule deer every fall and when my father, a sawmill worker, was laid off during economic downturns, he would poach deer to feed us. We had certain rituals important to the hunting of the deer. We gave thanks to the deer for offering themselves to us so we could eat. The liver of the deer, dressed with sage, was our first meal on the day it was killed. The mule deer, or black-tailed deer, is distinct from the smaller white-tailed deer found on the west side of the state.

Bagging a deer was a male initiation ritual. After the hunt, the deer was roped to the fender or hood of the pickup for the obligatory ride through town. A four-point (four antler points on one side of the rack) buck was considered a respectable kill while a two-point was not. Killing a spike (a young deer with one antler point on each side) was dishonorable. A true champion deer would have six or even eight points. Because the male deer sheds its antlers each year, the buck with more antlers was more mature and considered harder to hunt.

My father and I went to the winter range of the mule deer at the invitation of the game department. We travelled to the south end of Goose Lake, where literally thousands of deer came down from the Warner Mountains and ranges to the west to spend the winter in the grasslands near the lake. I was astonished at the numbers of deer we saw that weekend. The game department was concerned about overpopulation of the range and gave us bitterbrush seed to plant during our hunting trips to provide forage for the deer. Bitterbrush was one of the most nutritious browse plants for the deer of the Oregon desert herds. Later, hunting was opened for does to further reduce the population of deer. The population of deer greatly declined after these rule changes.

The mule deer makes seasonal migrations to find optimal browse conditions. The rut or mating season usually begins in the fall and males become more aggressive, competing for mates. Does may mate with more than one buck. The fawns born in the spring stay with their mothers during the summer and are weaned in the fall. Mule deer females usually give birth to two fawns.

Mountain lions are the mule deer's main natural predator in the Great Basin of Oregon. The lions, along with coyotes and bobcats, prey primarily on young or weak deer.

35. Muskrat

GROWING UP IN EASTERN OREGON, I had a friend whose trapper father mounted beaver and muskrat hides on thin boards to dry. Muskrats have been trapped since the first days of exploration and occupation of the West. They are commonly seen in Oregon's remote corner in wetlands, ponds, lakes, and along streams and rivers. Muskrats are not truly rats. They are rodents, but more closely related to voles and lemmings than to rats. The name probably comes from an Algonquin word *muscascus* meaning "it is red" or from the Abenaki word *moskwas.* The animal has a musky odor, and is larger than a rat but much smaller than a beaver.

Muskrat at Summer Lake refuge

Muskrats have short, thick fur with two layers to protect them from cold water. Their tails have scales and are flattened vertically for propulsion while swimming. They also have some webbing on their hind feet but they propel themselves mostly by the tail. Muskrats can dive underwater for ten to fifteen minutes and tolerate buildup of carbon dioxide. They can close off their ears to keep out water.

Muskrats are omnivorous but prefer plants like cattail and water lily. They also eat a small amount of meat from mussels, frogs, fish, and crayfish. They are food for mink, foxes, eagles, lynx, and coyotes. Muskrats do not store food for the winter like the pika.

Muskrats build lodges of plants and mud in marshes or burrow into banks with an entrance underwater. They live in male-female pairs with their young, and often fight over mates and territory.

Despite trapping and loss of habitat, the resilient muskrat is still with us in abundant numbers.

36. North American Porcupine

The North American porcupine is dark in color with white highlights. The only larger rodent is the American beaver. The porcupine has thousands of sharp, hollow, barbed quills that are modified hairs and used for defense. The porcupine does not throw its quills but it does use an ample tail to swat at threats. The quills feature barbs that make them very difficult to remove. (Our family dog, Mickey, found this out the hard way.) The porcupine is the only North American mammal with antibiotics in its skin in case it gets stuck with its own quills.

Porcupines often rest in trees. They do not hibernate but have a den to sleep in. They eat twigs, roots, stems, berries, conifer needles, and bark. Porcupines have poor sight and are slow moving. But they have an extraordinary ability to remember specific trees that are favorite foods.

One of my darkest days growing up was when the Forest Service had erroneously decided that porcupines were killing too many trees and offered a bounty on them. Our scout troop was driving home from a camping trip when we spotted a porcupine at the edge of the road. The troop jumped out, picked up rocks and began stoning the porcupine. The porcupine screamed and cried like a human baby in distress. I will never forget the sound of the porcupine pleading for its life. I have never forgiven myself for my part in stoning the porcupine.

37. Pacific Tree Frog

One spring day at Petroglyph Lake I saw something astonishing. The lake was in the process of drying, and a zone of mud cracks extended completely around its perimeter. As I walked along the edge, hundreds, then thousands, of tiny green and black frogs began to seep and ooze out of every crack in the mud. The proliferation of frogs continued around the entire lake perimeter. It was an amazing display of fecundity in a place as barren as an ephemeral lake on a sage flat with no trees or cover. There are years when the lake is completely dry, so these frogs must cuddle beneath dry cracked mud for months on end. Later in the day, I walked north to try to find an unnamed lake on the map. Temporarily lost, I found it by the cacophony of frog song drifting on a brisk north wind. It was likely that every drying lake on the Oregon desert was teeming with frogs that spring day.

Even though Petroglyph Lake is treeless, the frogs I saw that day were Pacific tree frogs. The frogs come in shades of green or brown or black and can change colors over periods of hours or weeks. They can be identified by a black eye stripe that stretches from the nose, over the eye and back to the shoulder. Their toes are long and slightly webbed, with sticky toe pads for climbing. The frog makes its home in a variety of habitats, not just woodlands, as shown by the frogs at Petroglyph Lake.

Tadpoles feed on algae, diatoms, and pollen in lakes and ponds, and metamorphosis takes four to six weeks. The tadpoles have four limbs and a tail. They stop feeding for a time and their digestive system changes from herbivorous to carnivorous. As adults they feed on spiders, beetles, flies, ants, and other insects. The predators of the frogs are herons, egrets, raccoons, snakes, and raptors. The frogs are nocturnal and their calls can be heard from very far away.

Pacific tree frogs are remarkable in that they are able to change colors, and they have a strong homing instinct and are able to find their way back to their home ponds.

The Pacific tree frog was named Washington's state amphibian. It is a keystone species in that other species depend on it for their survival.

38. Pika

THE PIKA LIVES IN ROCK PILES and talus slopes in the higher mountains of eastern Oregon. It shelters in the rocks but can also build burrows. A small mammal with short ears, no tail, and short limbs, it is sometimes called the "whistling hare" because of a high-pitched call it gives to warn of approaching predators. Pikas are territorial. Their predators include foxes, coyotes, hawks, eagles, and weasels.

The pika feeds on forbs, grasses, sedges, moss, and lichens. Pikas do not hibernate, so they harvest grass in the meadows near their rocky homes and make little haystacks to feed on during the winter. Pikas each make their own hay pile, which they will defend, but will also share with burrow mates. Pikas have incisors for gnawing and no canines, and are unusual because ovulation only occurs after copulation.

Pikas are adversely influenced by global climate change. As temperatures increase, they attempt to move to higher elevations. And, because they are located in mountains with specific arrangements of elevation, talus slopes, and meadows, their habitat islands make dispersal difficult. Several Great Basin populations have disappeared entirely. Pikas can still be found in the higher reaches of the Warner Mountains, Steens Mountains, and other higher ranges of the Oregon Outback.

39. Pronghorn Antelope

Once, when driving to the Sunstone Collection Area near Rabbit Hills, I got into a race with a pronghorn antelope (*Antilocapra americana*). The road was gravel but well graded so I could drive reasonably fast for desert country. The antelope won. Antelopes are the fastest land animals in the Western Hemisphere. They can run up to fifty-five miles per hour, and can sustain high speeds longer than cheetahs. Cheetah fossils have been found in Nevada, so throughout its evolutionary history, the antelope had to run for its life. The antelope's distinct stride measures eight yards. Adaptations for speed include large heart and lungs, hollow hair, and padded feet to absorb shock.

The antelope, however, is a not a good jumper and hence the effort on the Hart Mountain Antelope Refuge to remove all the barbed wire fence left over from the ranching era. By the 1920s the population of pronghorn in the western United States had declined to about 13,000, but thanks to conservation efforts as many as 1 million may now exist.

The namesake horn of the pronghorn antelope is actually a bone that is covered by a keratinous sheath that is shed and re-grown each year. The females have smaller horns, which are sometimes barely visible.

Antelope have a very wide field of vision—320 degrees—thanks to their prominent eyes. My father held the theory that antelope are curious and could be brought closer by waving a white cloth. (The antelope have white rumps so perhaps they were seeking company.) Antelopes can outsmart dogs. When my friend's dog encountered an antelope at a water hole, the dog took off chasing it. Of course the quicker antelope simply led the dog off into the desert to become coyote bait and circled back to the water hole.

The pronghorn is not really an antelope, systematically speaking. It does closely resemble the antelopes of the Old World and fills a similar ecological niche—an example of convergent evolution. During the Pleistocene twelve species existed in the family in North America. Only five existed when humans arrived and all are now extinct except for *Antilocapra americana*.

Pronghorn antelope at Hart Mountain Refuge

In the spring the antelope disband their mixed sex herds and the adult males lead a solitary life. Young males form bachelor bands. A mature pronghorn male is territorial and will maintain its territory by scent marking and vocalizing. Females will incite conflict between adult males and select the winning male and his territory. I have seen a male defend a harem of as many as a dozen females.

40. Redband Trout the Joy of Fly Fishing

If a Garden of Eden exists on the earth today, it would be—for me—a trout stream in the Oregon Outback. My favorite trout streams in the high desert of eastern Oregon are snowmelt- and spring-fed, cold, clear, and clean. They are swift and rocky in places and deep and languid and gravelly in others. Grasses, trees, and brush grow on the edge where the stream has cut back under the banks. Downed pine trees break up the water flow as does an occasional beaver dam constructed from quaking aspen. In the spring, wildflowers of every description give color to the banks while ducks float by and hawks patrol the sky.

The slack water behind rocks, the cut banks, and the grottoes beneath downed trees provide shelter for the wild fish of the stream—the redband trout. The redband trout are remnants of the last ice age when they became stranded in the upper reaches of streams that drained into huge glacial lakes. The lakes are just salt flats today, but the trout have lived on for ten thousand years surviving spring floods, drought, warm water, silt from overgrazing of the stream banks by cattle, and the introduction of non-native trout. The redband trout are wary and to catch them the angler must approach them with respect and grace.

Fly-fishing is a solitary sport—more meditative than competitive, more reclusive than social. Done properly it is as graceful as a ballet. The tools of the craft at their best are subtle and light. Favorite poles are lightweight and strong, made of graphite or bamboo. Reels are small and highly machined—smooth in action and precise in tolerance. Lines are lightweight, floating and tapered. Lures are made of threads, fabrics, hairs, and feathers with tiny barbless hooks. The flies float and some of them are miniscule. They mimic real insects but a certain latitude of creativity is permitted—a concession to the principle of what works.

Flies are named—some have names granted by legacy and tradition like those of a royal family—the Royal Coachman for instance. Many names are entomological like the plain "mosquito" or the "grasshopper." Other names are bestowed on flies that are designed for a specific river or stream or even a specific section of a river or stream.

Because the redband trout are survivors, they are naturally suspicious and cunning. The fisherman must make the fly drift down upon the water like an insect or cast it into the grass on the opposite side of the stream so that it bounces off and appears to fall directly from the grass. The fly must drift beneath the cut banks and rocks and tree branches in the river—not so close as to hang up but close enough to lure the trout out of hiding. If the trout does come out, it will be with the speed of lightning. There will be no time for the human eye to register the flash, transmit a command to the muscle, and set the hook. The good fly fisherman always leaves just the right tension in the drifting line to allow the striking trout to hook itself.

Fly-fishing requires a special sort of fluid grace—a grace that patterns itself after the flow of the stream. The smaller the stream the greater the hand and eye coordination required. On a small stream like those in eastern Oregon, sometimes a back cast is not even possible because of brush. The angler must learn to cast sideways, roll cast, or to back cast only in abbreviated arcs and angles. Casting must compensate for breezes and obstructions of all sorts in and over the water, yet take the fly to a precise spot on the riffle or pool.

Etiquette and aesthetic sense prevail on the fly stream. Live bait, sinking lines and lures, motor craft, barbed hooks, and keeping the fish are unwelcome. On good fly-fishing streams and lakes, all of these are illegal.

I like to think of fly-fishing as a metaphor for finding the wild spirits that inhabit nature. The spirits naturally try to hide. The successful seeker must go alone with a light touch and acrobatic poise and grace. The spirit must be lured out and, if caught, admired, and released alive.

Norman Maclean, in his book *A River Runs Through It*, describes the stream so well: "Eventually, all things merge into one, and a river runs through it. The river was cut by the world's great flood and runs over rocks from the basement of time. On some of the rocks are timeless raindrops. Under the rocks are the words, and some of the words are theirs. I am haunted by waters."

41. Western Fence Lizard

THE GREAT BASIN FENCE LIZARD is a subspecies of the western fence lizard. The fence lizard is brown to black in color with stripes on the back. Males have blue bellies and blue patches on the throat. The blue parts are often used in display to attract females or to intimidate other males. These lizards like to sun on rocks, walls, logs, and fence posts, where they are visible to predators such as hawks and some animals. But the lizards are as fast as blue lightning and that gives them a survival edge. They also have a detachable tail that can grow back.

The western fence lizard eats spiders and insects. During periods of extreme heat or cold the lizard becomes inactive and takes shelter under rocks, crevices, burrows, or tree bark. The cold-blooded lizard is most active on sunny days that are not too hot, and can be sluggish in the morning before the cold of the desert night dissipates. The lizard hibernates during the winter.

Lizards are a common depiction on petroglyphs in the Oregon high desert including Petroglyph Lake and Greaser Petroglyph. The lizards themselves are easy to see in the Oregon desert because they are not particularly shy and appear to be curious, stopping to observe for a few minutes before rapidly taking departure.

Halophytes and Crusts

42. Alkali Saltgrass ❧ Greasewood

Alkali saltgrass (genus *Distichlis*) and greasewood (genus *Sarcobatus*) are halophytes—salt tolerant plants—often found together on the alkali flats and playa lakeshores of the Oregon desert. When the salinity becomes too extreme, they give way to the even more salt-tolerant iodine bush.

A perennial, native plant, saltgrass grows on cracked salt flats with the rhizomes spreading from crack to crack in the hard ground. The rhizomes are sharply pointed and scaly to push through heavy clay soils. The grass can survive its salty environment because salt glands in the leaves extrude salt. It can also survive flooding as long as the leaves are exposed to air, and it can live on poorly drained soils. Saltgrass is also resistant to fire and trampling and is highly tolerant to direct sun.

Greasewood is a deciduous shrub that grows from two to nine feet tall. The plant is contains both male and female flowers, which appear from June to August. The plant reproduces from seeds inside small, winged fruit. Spiny branches ward off grazing animals, while the succulent leaves store water. (Greasewood also can cause oxalate poisoning and kidney failure in cattle and sheep.) Like alkali saltgrass, greasewood is found in sunny areas on the salt flats near playas. Native people and pioneers used the very hard wood for firewood. Greasewood was identified by the Lewis and Clark expedition of 1806.

Salt-tolerant grass

Greasewood and saltgrass demonstrate the adaptability and struggle for life in the desert. They are survivors.

43. Desert Varnish

Petroglyph carved in desert varnish

DESERT VARNISH is a thin, dark brown to black coating on exposed basalt rocks in the arid areas of the remote quarter. Varnish is primarily wind-deposited clay with iron and manganese oxides. Some scientists think that the desert varnish in cross-section resembles stromatolites—layers formed by generations of bacteria (Toomey 2013). Desert varnish may have been produced by organisms that concentrate minerals like manganese and iron not typically found in rocks with desert varnish. Manganese in black desert varnish is fifty to sixty times more abundant than in rocks in the earth's crust (Dorn and Oberlander 1981). The enrichment is thought to be due to the work of manganese-oxidizing microbes found in organic-poor substrates.

So far scientists have been unable to reproduce the varnish in the lab using bacteria but some scientists maintain that the varnish represents the work of extremophiles with complex chemistry. If this is the case, the desert varnish represents the outer boundaries of life as we know it (Toomey 2013). Desert varnish remains a mystery.

Naturalist Charles Darwin on his voyage on the HMS *Beagle* discovered rocks that appeared "burnished" on the coast of South America near San Salvador. He deduced that the rocks glittered because of thin layers of metallic oxides but he could not explain how they got there (Toomey 2013).

Desert varnish in the Oregon remote quarter was essential to petroglyph art produced by Native Americans. Scratched or carved through the thin varnish layer, the designs of the petroglyphs stand out when lighter colored rocks are exposed beneath the varnish. Evidently desert varnish takes a great deal of time to redevelop once removed because some of the petroglyphs at Long Lake have been dated to before 6,600 years BP. Some of these petroglyphs are buried beneath Mount Mazama (Crater Lake) ash.

Desert varnish is just one of the many peculiar features to be found in the Oregon desert—a number of them still wrapped in mystery.

44. Diatoms

IN THE OREGON DESERT there are beds of diatomaceous earth such as those at Christmas Valley. The huge lakes of the Pleistocene era were filled with diatoms (algae, or phytoplankton), as the much smaller remnant lakes are today. Over thousands of years, the remains of the diatoms piled up to form deep beds of solid diatomaceous earth, which today is mined and used to make absorbents, abrasives, filtration materials, and insulators.

There are at least 100,000 species of diatoms—algae (phytoplankton)—that have been on the earth for 144 million years. They live in the seas, lakes, soils, rivers, and ponds of the world as single cells, filament, or colonies, drifting at the mercy of wind, tide, and current. Because diatoms are photosynthetic and use carbon dioxide while releasing oxygen as a waste product, they were instrumental in conditioning the early atmosphere of the earth, making it suitable for animal life. The Herculean task of creating the living atmosphere of the earth was accomplished by organisms so small that they were not properly described until the advent of the microscope. Today diatoms account for 45 percent of the primary organic production on the earth including much of the oxygen.

Not only are diatoms small, they are beautiful. Diatoms are symmetrical and made of tiny shells called valves that are made of organic materials impregnated with silica. In other words, they are glass. The shells are intricate and elaborate with patterns like tiny etchings made by a master jeweler. The glass cases house the chlorophyll and soft cell parts of the diatoms, protecting them while concentrating the light necessary for photosynthesis. Looking at diatoms under a microscope is like studying intricate, colorful snowflakes.

45. Lichens & Other Xerophytes

ASTONISHING PLANTS AND ANIMALS live on the high desert: plants able to grow on solid rock faces, miniature flowers that bloom on rim rock shelves and rock flats with no apparent soil, tiny organisms that thrive in hot springs and brines saltier than the ocean. How can living things survive such extremes of hot and cold, wet and dry, brine and fresh, rock and sand, calm and wind blast? I can think of a no more demanding home.

The bright red lichens near the shore of Lake Abert manage to thrive on bare basalt rock faces directly exposed to intense, high altitude sun as well as incessant drying winds that can bring bitter cold one hour and scorching heat the next. Pablo Neruda, in his poem "Stones from the Sky," expresses the primordial quality of lichen: "The lichen on the stone/mesh of green elastic/enmeshes the primal hieroglyph/stretches the scripture of the sea around the round rock."

Almost as amazing as the lichens are the tiny desert flowers that bloom on the lithosol or rock-soil of the desert. The lithosol develops in areas underlain by basalt. Not even sage grows well there. Wherever even a teaspoon of soil accumulates between rock fragments, the

Lichens on rocks near Lake Abert

flowers, some almost microscopic, bloom in a wet spring. The plants need to be small and close to the ground to survive the drying wind and lack of water on the lithosol.

In general, arid zone plants or xerophytes exhibit a number of adaptations: very strong osmotic or water sucking potential due to high internal salt concentrations; waxy coating called cuticles to save water loss; hairy leaves to reduce air movement and evaporation over the leaves; the ability to close stomata (the openings beneath the leaves) during the day to conserve water; reduction of leaf area compared to leaf volume; and the capacity to store water in the plant structures. Some desert plants like the purple sage and juniper release a toxin from the decaying material they shed to prevent other plants from growing under or near them. Why allow competitors to take precious water? This advantage, along with a shallow and wide-spreading root system and deep tap root system, enables the plants to harvest water from brief and infrequent storms, and extract water from deep in the ground.

The saline zone near alkali playa lakes is even more extreme for plant growth than the lithosol zone. Here the plants must also adapt to high salt concentrations. Extreme salt tolerant plants such shadscale, greasewood, and saltgrass, the true halophyte, grow where no other plants can; they do it by maintaining very high internal salt concentrations.

Tiny crustaceans called brine shrimp thrive in the salty waters of Lake Abert, a lake much saltier than the sea. Some years they are so prolific that their tiny brown eggs or cysts float in visible rafts on the lake waters. The sexually produced cysts are so resistant to drying that they have survived in lab beakers full of dry mud for fifteen years only to bounce back to life when water is added. These tiny shrimp feed by filtering plankton and algae from the water, swim by waving their tiny articulated appendages, and respire by removing oxygen from the salt water through their body wall. The shrimp are clear organisms, but they change color to match the color of their latest meal. The proliferation of high protein brine shrimp in Lake Abert has not gone unnoticed by flocks of thousands of migrating birds including avocets, grebes, phalaropes, and plovers.

The wild living entities of the natural world are alive and well in the Oregon desert; not even the hardest rock, the saltiest water, the driest wind or the longest drought can deter their ingenious proliferation.

46. Iodine Bush

The iodine bush—*Allenrolfia occidentalis*—was named after botanist Allen Rolfe of Kew Gardens in London. The name "iodine" probably comes from the brown color of the crushed leaves. It is a halophyte that grows in extremely saline soils. The shrub forms hummocks by collecting windblown sand. Underground runners assist in the spread of the plant, although its flowers have both stamen and pistils and are wind pollinated. The branches are segmented, scale-like, and green. The plant grows up to three feet high.

Unlike some other halophytes that secrete salts, iodine bush stores water to dilute the salts. Salt diffuses into the roots from the playa soil and is exported from the cells by a chemical pumping mechanism using photosynthesis as the energy source (Mozingo 1987).

Few animals eat iodine bush because of salty stems. However it is one of the most common plants on the playas. It is found on the coasts of the Mediterranean, Caspian, and Red Seas and on the steppes of Central Asia as well as the playas of the American West. This hardy bush has adapted to life in an extreme environment that very few other plants can tolerate.

47. Microbiotic Crust (Cryptogams)

A MICROBIOTIC CRUST is a dark, spongy crust on the ground in the semi-arid and arid lands of the Oregon steppe. It can cover from 10 to 100 percent of the exposed ground. Many of the crusts on alkali flats growing near or under sagebrush appear black. A well-developed crust indicates a healthy desert ecology. The crust serves to anchor the soil from wind and runoff, stores water, and assists in decomposition of biotic debris on the desert floor.

The microbiotic crust is essentially a living, organic soil that is made up of a combination of cyanobacteria (single-celled photosynthetic bacteria), algae, fungi, lichens, and bryophytes (mosses). The different plants that make up the crust act symbiotically to photosynthesize (algae), recycle waste (fungi), and store water (moss). Lichens are a component of the crust and they themselves represent a symbiotic relationship between algae and fungi. The microbiotic crust is fragile and easily damaged by human or animal foot traffic, off-road vehicles, and cheatgrass fires, requiring many years if not decades to recover. Because of their importance to desert health, more research and restoration attention is being given to the microbiotic crusts.

Microbiotic crusts are often referred to as cryptogams, plants that reproduce as spores. The name derives from the Greek words *kryptos,* meaning hidden, and *gameein,* meaning reproduction. Linnaeus divided the plant kingdom into twenty-five classes, one of which was *Crytpgamia.* However recent advances in systematics have placed some of the cryptogams outside of the plant kingdom. Fungi are now more closely related to animals than plants and some algae are allied with bacteria. The term cryptogam still has some utility to mean a complex of organisms functioning together in a difficult environment to augment each other.

Desert visitors should avoid stepping on the dark, spongy, and fragile crusts whenever possible.

Birds

48. American Avocet

American avocet at Lake Abert

THE AMERICAN AVOCET frequents the shores of playa lakes, mud flats, and alkali flats in the remote corner of Oregon. The migratory birds gather by the hundreds on the east shore of Lake Abert and are summer residents throughout the Great Basin.

The avocet has black and white coloring, a cinnamon colored head, and long, thin bill upturned at the end. It has long legs well suited to wading in shallow water and webbed feet that help it walk on soft mud or swim offshore.

The bill seems ungainly for feeding but it is deployed as a scythe, sweeping from side to side to filter brine shrimp, brine flies, and crustaceans out of the water, or to scrape food off the mud. The bird can grab insects from the air or forage in a cooperative manner by forming a phalanx with other avocets, wading forward shoulder to shoulder.

Avocets may engage in a group dance during mating season. They form a circle and, standing next to their mate, stretch their beaks forward parallel to the water with necks extended. They move one direction and then the other in the circle. Avocets also engage in pre-copulation displays that involve breast preening. Sometimes the preening movement is so rapid that the birds splash water high in the air.

Avocets nest in colonies near water—on islands or marshy shorelines—to avoid predators. They make their nests simply by scraping a space on the ground and use little nesting material. Both sexes incubate the eggs, but the young are able to leave the nest and feed themselves within a few hours of hatching. When the parents exchange incubation duties, the departing parent will ceremonially pick up small objects and toss them over back in the direction of the nest (Ryser 1985). Avocets will also engage in distraction displays, diving or feigning injury if the colony is approached by intruders. The colorful and anatomically unusual avocet represents a remarkable adaptation to a challenging habitat.

49. California Quail

THE MALE CALIFORNIA QUAIL is the perfect little father and gentleman. He will often strike a pompous pose with his colorful mottled gold chest sticking out and a rakish little plume of feathers or topknot hanging out from over his eyes. Quails perch on fence posts chirping their status calls and will change the call if they spot a cat or other threat. In the meantime, the covey on the ground below scratch away at the ground to get seeds or other morsels from the soil. Their diet consists of seeds, leaves, berries, and some insects.

Quails are very social animals and have communal dust baths where they burrow down into the soil, ruffle their feathers, flap their wings, and toss dirt in the air. Family groups join together into communal broods including at least two females, multiple males, and many offspring.

As a youngster I hunted quail with my friends. When we got too close, they would explode into the air, often rattling us so much that it spoiled our aim. Quail are very fast on their feet and it is amusing to watch the covey run across a road. The quail of my youth lived along roads or in fields or sagebrush flats, but it was not unusual for them to visit our garden. They are very adaptable and even in urban areas it is not unusual to hear the call of the male looking over the covey or to see a covey beat feet across a road. Some neighborhoods even have quail crossing street signs.

Somehow, as long as there are quail, everything seems right with the world.

50. Dipper

The dipper, also called the water ouzel, is an unremarkable bird in color and appearance: dark brown or nearly black, with a short tail, short wings, and a small body.

I have often seen dippers on cold, fast moving mountain streams in the Fremont National Forest. They can also be found on Steens Mountain and the Warner Mountains. Dippers like the shady reaches of mountain streams, so they are sometimes hard to see. However, their dipping, bobbing motion gives them away. Their loud, high-pitched call can be heard above the flow of a stream. They also communicate visually by blinking to show the pale upper eyelids in a series of white flashes.

Some people say that the dipper can "fly" underwater, and while this may seem to be an exaggeration, they are well suited for underwater feeding. Their short, strong wings can be used like flippers to help them move in the water where they reach down to feed on nymphs, stoneflies, caddisflies, mayflies, small fish, crustaceans, and mollusks.

Dippers do not have webbed feet but have long legs and sharp claws to help them grip underwater. They have nasal flaps and high hemoglobin concentrations in the blood that store oxygen. Even their eyes are adapted to underwater vision. Their down is similar to that of geese and ducks, and provides insulation in the cold waters.

Dippers nest in globe-shaped structures with side entrances near stream banks or under waterfalls. Their nests are layered so that the inner grass remains dry. The male helps feed the young. Dippers are good indicators of water quality since they do not reside in polluted or silted streams.

51. Killdeer

THE KILLDEER (*Charadrius vociferous*) has always been one of my favorite birds. With its distinctive red eye circles and black and white markings, killdeer are a common site on the gravel and sand bars of the remote quarter's streams. The adults are known for feigning a broken wing while giving its loud, peculiar cry to lure predators away from the nest.

The eggs are so well camouflaged on the ground that it is difficult to find them—but also easy to step on them unknowingly. The nest is an example of minimalist architecture; it is not much more than bowl on the ground camouflaged with some stones and grass. The eggs are speckled to closely resemble their surroundings. The young are precocial—able to see and forage soon after hatching.

Killdeer frequent pastures, meadows, and fields, as well as stream banks. They like to eat insects and are no doubt instrumental in keeping grasshoppers and mosquitoes under control. Killdeer have adapted well to development and are able to exploit agricultural and suburban habitat. They are migratory, travelling as far as South America. Look for them on Deep Creek, Dairy Creek, the Chewaucan River, Summer Lake Refuge, and Lake Abert.

52. Mountain Bluebird

When I think of migratory birds in the Oregon high desert, my thoughts naturally turn to the plethora of ducks, geese, and shorebirds that migrate on the Pacific Flyway, stopping at the many playa lakes, wetlands, and refuges along the way. But of course smaller birds migrate through the high desert as well, and some even stop to nest. During summer it is not unusual to see a bright blue bird flitting from sagebrush to sagebrush. The mountain bluebird prefers elevations about 5,000 feet, and much of the high desert meets that criteria.

The male mountain bluebird is bright turquoise-blue with a lighter underside. The female has duller blue wings and tail and a grey throat, breast, crown, and back. The bluebird migrates from Mexico to Alaska, and some stop in Oregon for the summer. They survive on insects and berries, and the grasshoppers of the desert no doubt provide a major portion of their diet.

Bluebirds are monogamous, and the males sing when the sun rises. Females build the nests, but both males and females fiercely protect it. The young are helpless at hatching and take twenty-one days before leaving the nest.

Mountain bluebirds are not endangered because so many people in the West build bird boxes for them. The bird prefers to cavity nest so the boxes greatly assist the species. But enough of the beautiful birds like the solitude of the desert well enough to provide a splash of color in the muted landscape.

53. Red-winged Blackbird

WHEN GROWING UP in the Outback, I could always tell that spring had arrived when the red-winged blackbird (*Agelaius phoeniceus*) males established their territories with their distinctive "okkalleeeoooo" calls. Before long the males would be evenly spaced in the willow trees along the stream bank or pond shore.

This blackbird is sexually dimorphic: the male is black and has brightly colored red and yellow epaulets, while the female is drab brown. The genus name is derived from the ancient Greek word *agelaius,* "belonging to a flock," while the species name, *phoeniceus,* is from the Latin meaning "deep red." Males will aggressively defend their territories even to the point of suicide missions. They will defend many females even though the females manage to copulate with other males, resulting in mixed clutches.

The primary enemies of the red-winged blackbirds are raptors. Crows, ravens, magpies, herons, raccoons, foxes, and snakes predate the eggs. Red-wings protect themselves by nesting in groups and over water, with alarm calls, and by mobbing predators. Blackbird nests are made of cattails, rushes, and willows lined with moss, sedge, grass, and mud. These birds can often be seen clinging sideways to a cattail stem while swaying in the breeze.

I am very fond of the calls of the male red-wings as a sign of spring. I like how they fly along from tree to tree or cattail to cattail to accompany me on my walks—perhaps out of curiosity, a desire to escort me out of their territory, or both.

54. Sandhill Crane

As a youngster growing up in the Oregon desert, I felt there was no more mournful sound than the distant call of a flock of sandhill cranes. In the spring I could always hear them before I saw them. They flew very high up, even higher than geese, and seemed to take their time, stopping along the way to circle in thermals. Their wingspans of up to seven feet make them natural soaring birds.

Mated pairs of cranes call in unison in a duet, though the female makes more calls than the male.

The sandhill crane has a distinctive red forehead with white cheeks and a long pointed bill. They have long necks and legs that stretch out straight during flight. While a huge number migrate by way of the Nebraska sandhills, they are common in the remote corner of Oregon, where they nest in fields or in the wetlands of refuges such as Summer Lake.

The sandhill crane has one of the longest fossil histories among birds still found today. A sandhill crane fossil from Nebraska is possibly 10 million years old.

Sandhill cranes are social birds usually found in pairs or family groups, and sometimes in large congregations. The cranes feed on seeds, including cultivated plants like corn and wheat, as well as insects, snails, berries, and small reptiles and amphibians. Both parents incubate the eggs and the young are hatched with eyes open, able to leave the nest within two days. Extended care is provided to the young for up to ten months after hatching. Cranes can live as long as twenty-one years.

Predators include foxes, coyotes, bobcats, hawks, eagles, and owls, with the young cranes being most vulnerable. Cranes will defend themselves aggressively, stabbing with their bills and flailing with their wings.

At Summer Lake Refuge I was privileged to witness two cranes dancing. It was not mating season, but the dances can occur any time of year, although usually during breeding season. The cranes jumped in unison, flapped their wings, and bowed to each other in a very choreographed display.

55. White Pelican

Pelicans love soaring in thermals and playing in water. I have often observed a flock of them circling in the air near the headquarters of Malheur Refuge. They drift along in the thermal, rarely finding the need to flap their wings to maintain altitude. I have also observed a flock of pelicans at Hart Lake at the foot of Hart Mountain drifting down the rapids where the lake has an outlet to the Warner wetlands. The birds would drift down the quarter-mile water chute, then fly back up to the lake, and go down again and again.

The white pelican (*Pelecanus erythrorhynchos*) is named from the Latin term for pelican *Pelecanus* and the ancient Greek word *erythrorhynchos* meaning red nose. Only the California condor has a larger wingspan than the white pelican. The pelican is remarkable for its large bill and throat sac that is vivid orange during breeding season. There is also a flat horn on the upper bill that is shed after the birds have laid their eggs. Pelicans have large webbed feet and are excellent swimmers.

Pelicans operate in groups of a dozen or so to corral fish and feed. Unlike the brown pelican, white pelicans do not dive for food but fish while swimming. They fish for whatever species are available but will travel far to find better fishing grounds. Pelicans are also known to steal fish from other birds such as gulls and cormorants.

Pelicans are often seen in flocks and breed in colonies. Their nests are shallow depressions lined with twigs, sticks, and reeds. Both parents incubate the clutch of up to six eggs for about a month. After hatching the young stay in the nest, although usually only one survives. The young spend another month in a pod, molting mature plumage and learning to fly. The parents care for the young until the family bond is broken in late summer or early fall as the migration to winter habitat begins.

When travelling near the many playa lakes, it is fascinating to watch the pelican soar in seemingly endless invisible columns of warm air rising as the desert sun heats up the salt flats. The graceful flight of the pelican adds beauty to the remote landscape.

61. The Pleistocene Era

THE GEOLOGIC PLEISTOCENE ERA brought to Oregon's remote corner dramatic changes in flora, fauna, climate, geology, and native cultures. The era extended from about 2.6 million years ago to about 12,000 years ago, and included eleven glacial periods. The era corresponds to the Paleolithic age in archaeology.

During the Pleistocene repeated continental glacial cycles reached as far south as the 40th parallel (a line that runs across the United States from the mid-Atlantic through northern California). Perhaps as much as 30 percent of the earth was covered by sheets of ice as thick as 5,000 to almost 10,000 feet. Sea levels dropped 300 feet over the entire earth. During this period, mountain glaciers carved cirques and U-shaped canyons on Steens Mountain, Gearhart Mountain, and Warner Mountains. When the large ice sheets began to retreat and the climate began to warm, large, deep pluvial lakes formed (Flint 1957). Ancient shorelines from these lakes are still clearly visible on slopes throughout the Oregon desert.

Many large mammals, mammoths, mastodons, saber-tooth cats, ground sloths, horses, camels, and cave bears went extinct during this period. Some of these are preserved as fossils found at Fossil Lake near Lost Forest. During the Pleistocene humans began to use more sophisticated tools. During the ice ages and afterward, humans expanded their range throughout the world. Artifacts found at Fort Rock and Paisley Caves indicate human habitation near current day Summer Lake as far back as 14,000 years or more. Current theories contend that humans arrived in North America by way of a Bering Strait land bridge when sea levels were lower, or that humans used vessels to travel down coast lines to the tip of South America. As the pluvial lakes began to dry, the peoples of current eastern Oregon adopted a more hunting-gathering lifestyle as opposed to the more settled Chewaucan culture centered on the shores of current Lake Abert (Pettigrew 1985).

As the pluvial lakes retreated and the climate became drier, the changes to native cultures must have been significant. I found one possible indication of this at a cupule site on the shore of current Hart

Lake. The site features a boulder in which small cups—about one-and-a-quarter inch across and half an inch deep—are carved. There is also a stone circle, probably the foundation of a habitation, and an overhang with soot on the roof. Some archaeologists think that cupules may have been played a role in attempts by shamans to bring rain.

62. Pluvial Lakes

A PLUVIAL LAKE is a landlocked basin filled with water during glacial periods when rainfall is high. The word comes from the Latin *pluvia,* meaning rain. If the climate changes and the lake dries out, it is known as a playa or alkali flat. In the Pleistocene era, a number of large, deep lakes occupied what is now the Oregon desert. The remnants of the lakes today—the playa lakes—occupy the grabens in horst and graben fault-block topography. The terrain today is endorheic, meaning there is no drainage to the sea. Because of the lack of drainage, the salinity levels are very high in many of the remnant lakes.

The major Pleistocene pluvial lakes in Oregon's southeast corner were Silver/Christmas/Fossil, Chewaucan, Harney/Malheur, Warner, Guano/Alvord, Mann, Goose, and Klamath/Tule. The largest pluvial lake in the Great Basin was Lake Bonneville—now known as the Great Salt Lake in Utah. One of the most notable pluvial lakes in Oregon's remote corner was Lake Chewaucan—a 480-square-mile lake encompassing present day Lake Abert, Summer Lake, and the Chewaucan marsh (Allison 1982). The lake reached a depth of 375 feet and lake terraces are clearly visible on the slopes surrounding the playa lakes today.

Summer Lake—the remnant of a pluvial lake—seen from Winter Ridge

63. Vernal Pools

'ernal pool at Hart Mountain

A VERNAL POOL is an ephemeral body of water, usually devoid of fish, that dries in the spring and summer with distinctive bands of vegetation and flowers around the margins, which change as the pond dries. Seen from above, the ponds can vary in color from red to gold to orange to black, with a rainbow of colors in bands around the pool. Petroglyph Lake is an example of a somewhat larger vernal pool.

The vernal pools can begin the summer full of water from rainfall, snowmelt, or runoff but evapotranspiration in the high desert climate begins the drying process. Some pools may retain some water throughout the year but others completely dry up. Large playa lakes, such as Lake Abert, do not fit the definition of vernal pools because they have higher concentrations of dissolved minerals.

When full of water or early in the process of drying, vernal pools may teem with life, hosting some species of frogs and a variety of plants and flowers. At Petroglyph Lake I have witnessed thousands of tiny brown and black frogs oozing out of the mud cracks on the edge of the drying lake. Vernal pools are often underlain with hardpans or silts and clays to retain the water.

Distinctive zones of plant species occur at the edge of a vernal pool as it dries, because of seasonal gradients of moisture, salinity, and competition. Some of the species have buried seeds that accumulate in the soil. Little or no research has been done on Oregon steppe vernal pools, but about 80 percent of the plants in California vernal pools are annuals. A California pool typically hosts about fifteen to twenty—although sometimes up to one hundred—species of vascular plants. Vernal pools host a number of rare or threatened species of endemic plants and animals. Some species of vernal pool inhabitants, like the fairy shrimp, enter a state of cryptobiosis (or dormancy) and hatch only when rains recharge the pool with water. Some amphibians spend their entire life cycle within one hundred feet of a specific vernal pool. Each pool can have a distinctive assemblage of flora.

Vernal pools are paradoxical. They themselves are ephemeral, temporary—yet they harbor plants and animals that can survive over long periods of time and are found nowhere else.

Atmospherics

64. Dust Devils

Dust devils are a common sight on the alkali flats, sage flats, and grasslands of the Oregon steppe, particularly in the spring and summer. Whirlwinds ranging from a few feet to one hundred feet in diameter, dust devils can be over 3,000 feet tall and reach wind speeds of forty-five miles per hour. (Some can even reach sixty miles per hour with a diameter of 300 feet, and can last up to twenty minutes.) Dust devils are vertical rotating columns of air that are not nearly as damaging or powerful as a tornado.

Dust devils rarely cause injuries, but I know from personal experience that they can sting and a person caught in one will get covered in dirt. The Navajo called them *chiindii*—ghosts or spirits of dead Navajos. If a chiindii spins clockwise, it is a good spirit but if it spins counterclockwise, it is a bad spirit. (Unlike tornados, dust devils spin in both directions.)

Dust devil on Summer Lake

Dust devils form when hot air rises from the land in a rising and expanding thermal. Flat, barren terrain, or desert flats increase the likelihood of devil formation. Clear skies help the ground surface absorb solar energy to heat the air. Light wind is also essential since higher winds destabilize the spinning motion. Dust devils can produce radio noise and generate electrical fields due to the static effect of bumping particles.

Viking orbiters photographed dust devils on Mars in the 1970s as part of NASA's space exploration program. These photos showed that Martian dust devils can be fifty times wider and ten times as high as those seen on Earth.

65. Lenticular Clouds

Lenticular clouds over Long Lake

LENTICULAR CLOUDS are layered, stationary, lens-shaped clouds that often appear as caps on mountains or downwind of mountain ranges. They are very high clouds, up to 40,000 feet in altitude. Because the Cascade Range is west of the Oregon remote quarter, the lenticular clouds are often seen extending eastward in the jet stream, flowing from the west. The clouds form when air rising over mountains cools to the dew point, causing the vapor to condense and become visible. Sometimes the lenticular clouds stack up in layers like plates. The air descending into the trough between the waves can also warm up and re-evaporate to form cloud waves. Clouds can also form away from mountains along a weather front.

Lenticular clouds can be turbulent so pilots avoid them, but glider pilots seek them out. Gliders use the wave lift to gain remarkable altitudes and travel great distances. Because of their peculiar, saucer-like shape, lenticular clouds have sometimes been mistaken for UFOs.

66. Virga

VIRGA IS A STREAK OR SHAFT of precipitation that falls from a cloud base but does not reach the ground. As ice crystals or rain fall from high altitude clouds, heating due to compression causes the evaporation or sublimation of the water or ice respectively.

Virga can assist in seeding storm cells when small particles are blown into supersaturated air and act as condensation nuclei. This enables thunderhead clouds to form.

Dry microbursts occur when rain falls from a cloud base and mixes with dry air. As the rain evaporates the surrounding air is cooled due to the latent heat of evaporation of water. Energy is needed to overcome the molecular forces of attraction between water molecules and this heat comes from the surrounding air, causing it to cool. When the cool air reaches the ground it spreads out in all directions. Microbursts can be very hazardous to aircraft, particularly when landing, due the wind shear and falling air currents.

Goose Lake virga

Trees and Flowers

67. Alder

ALDERS GROW UP TO thirty feet high along the stream banks of the Oregon desert. Along with birch, cottonwoods, and willows, the alder is a riparian species with an important role in stream bank stability. The alder's shallow, spreading root system is well adapted to wet soil. The tree also provides seeds and habitat for small birds.

Alders reproduce via catkins. The male catkins grow in clusters up to three inches long. The female catkins are woody and cone-like and also grow in clusters. Alders are notable for their nitrogen-fixing abilities. Spherical nodules containing nitrogen-fixing bacteria are found on alder roots. The nodules take free nitrogen from the air and fix it for use by the alder. Nitrogen is also released to the soil water as alder leaves, roots, and trunks decay, thus playing a role in the nutrition of the entire riparian zone. This phenomenon also improves phytoplankton production in streams and ponds leading to more insects and feed for fish.

Along with the mountain alder of the Oregon remote quarter, there are many species of alder with many uses. Most of the pilings that form the foundation of Venice were made from alder trees. Alder bark contains the anti-inflammatory salicin. Native Americans used red alder bark to treat poison oak, insect bites, and skin irritations. Electric guitars have been built with alder bodies since the 1950s. As a hardwood, alder is used in making furniture, cabinets, and other wood products.

For the semi-arid and arid steppe of Oregon, riparian zones are crucial for providing bird, animal, and insect habitat; buffering spring floods; producing shade and food for fish; and preventing bank erosion and stream sedimentation.

68. Big Sagebrush

BIG SAGEBRUSH (*Artemisia tridentata*) is a grey shrub with yellow flowers and silvery foliage. It can grow up to ten feet tall and puts down tap roots that can go thirteen feet deep. Sagebrush also has a spreading root system near the surface so that the plant can obtain water from surface rain and snowmelt, as well as from groundwater tables. Big sagebrush can live more than 100 years in part because of its strong, pungent odor that discourages browsing.

Sagebrush is an evergreen and flowers in late summer or early fall. It can also reproduce through sprouts that come up from an underground rhizome. The seedling method of reproduction is more problematic since the seedlings need moisture for germination while the sprouts for rhizomes come from already established plants.

Big sagebrush and other species in the genus *Artemisia* are dominant plants throughout the Great Basin (big sagebrush is the state

Corral and sagebrush

flower of Nevada). However, big sagebrush habitat has declined rapidly in key parts of its range due to livestock grazing, invasive plant species, conversion to agricultural land, and climate change. For instance, big sagebrush has declined in 99 percent of its range in the Columbia Basin. Large areas of sagebrush were burned to establish grazing land, which invited invasive plants like cheatgrass to alter the ecosystem. Cheatgrass burns readily and can reestablish itself quickly after a fire. More frequent fires in cheatgrass areas prevented regrowth of sagebrush. Some tree species can also displace sagebrush as in the Warner Mountains where it has been outcompeted by California white fir.

Big sagebrush provides food and habitat for sage grouse, pronghorn antelope, pygmy rabbits, and mule deer. Sage grouse and Columbia Basin Pygmy Rabbit habitat are of particular concern due the declines in these species.

The plant was used by Native Americans to prevent infection, stop internal bleeding, and treat colds. The active ingredients include terpenoids, camphor, and tannins.

Big sagebrush has a unique method of communication with other plants of the species. Grazing herbivores can cause the plants to release volatile chemicals that signal nearby plants. If the terpenoid oils reach high enough concentrations they are toxic to the symbiotic bacteria in the stomachs of some animals like deer and cattle. The plant-to-plant communication via volatile chemicals can alert nearby plants to increase the repellent compounds at their disposal. The pronghorn antelope is the only large herbivore that can graze the sagebrush extensively.

The leaves are covered with a dense layer of short hairs (Mozingo 1987), which gives big sagebrush its silvery appearance. The hairs may help the plant to reduce water loss. Another interesting adaptation is the cork layer beneath each annual ring of woody tissue (Monzingo 1987). In most woody plants the cork forms only outside the woody tissues on the outside of the bark. Because big sagebrush has cork in each annual growth layer, the plant is more resistant to drying and invasion by fungi, bacteria, and animal damage.

69. Camas

Camas (*Camassia)* grows in wild, moist meadows in the Oregon Outback. Where I grew up in Lakeview, Oregon, there were vast meadows of purple camas flowers each spring in the wetlands near our house. Today the meadows have given way to farmland and human dwellings. But I can still see a camas meadow after dropping off the summit of Warner Pass on Highway 140 heading east towards Adel—a place called Camas Prairie on the map. Camas is a perennial plant used by Native Americans as a food source. (There is a toxic species of death camas with white flowers, but it is in a different genus.) The edible, nutritious bulbs were dug up and pit roasted or boiled. Dried bulbs were ground into flour. Gathering camas bulbs is still a tradition for many tribes. Camas spreads by seeds and not by runners.

A specific species called Cusick's camas (*Camassia cuskickii*) is found in eastern Oregon.

70. Native Wild Plum

The native wild plum, *Prunus subcordata,* also called Oregon plum, Sierra plum, or Klamath plum, grows in abundance in Lake and Klamath Counties in Oregon and in Modoc County in northern California. Along the entire range of the Warner Mountains at elevations of four to seven thousand feet, the plums grow in thickets along streams or in canyons and on the shorelines of ancient pluvial lakes. The scrubby trees or shrubs, six or more feet tall, produce ripe fruit the size of cherries. The plum sprouts from its roots and it is tolerant of extremes in heat, cold, alkaline soils, and drought.

John Work, while exploring for the Hudson's Bay Company near Goose Lake, reported in his journal killing a deer and eating a delicious fruit he named the wild plum. In 1843 another explorer, Captain Lassen, found the plum on his trip to California. The natives of the region dried the fruit and used it to flavor their game and wild fowl. In their journals, pioneers descending the Warner Mountains into Goose Lake valley also report finding and relishing the wild plums in the late summer and early fall.

Each fall my family would explore the foothills and draws of the Warner Mountains overlooking Goose Lake to pick wild plums by the bucketful. My mother canned the fruit for jams. When we had fresh deer meat or goose, they were flavored with wild plums. The fruit can be tart, but at the peak of ripeness the plums are sweet enough to eat by the handful. Today, near the town of New Pine Creek on the west slope of the Warner Mountain near the shores of Goose Lake, an orchard operation grows and processes wild plums to make jam, syrup, and wine. I have not developed a taste for the wine but the delicious syrup and jam remind me of my childhood.

71. Ponderosa Pine

WHERE I GREW UP in the southeast Oregon town of Lakeview, sawmills and box factories turned out ponderosa pine lumber and wooden boxes that filled long trains of freight cars. For a time in the 1940s and 1950s, the pine forests of eastern Oregon produced more lumber than the better-watered fir forests on the western side of the state. Today there are few uncut old-growth groves of ponderosa pine left. Only one sawmill remains in Lakeview, and the days of a logging truck carrying only one immense log to the mill are gone. The sawmill has been retooled to cut much smaller logs. Ponderosa pines still tower over the Oregon steppe, growing in the higher reaches of the Warner Mountains, the high lands west of Winter Ridge and the headwaters of the Chewaucan River, and Gearhart Mountain. It is noticeably absent on Steens Mountain.

The ponderosa pine is a coniferous evergreen tree. Its distinctive bark can appear to glow an orange color in the morning or afternoon light. Ponderosa pine trees can become quite large. The National Register of Big Trees lists one that is 235 feet tall and 324 inches in circumference from the Siskiyou National Forest. The oldest known Ponderosa on record was a fallen tree in Colorado dated at 1,047 years old.

Ponderosa pines can put down taproots of five to six feet. They have a distinctive three-needle cluster up to fifteen inches long. The female and male cones are separate and the cones have a tiny spine on each scale making them prickly to the touch.

A healthy stand of ponderosa pine has a clean floor underneath with little litter. The pine depends on periodic fires to clear the deep litter of needles and humus so that seedlings can take root. Under natural conditions fires would clean the ground beneath a grove every four to ten years. Without fire, shade-tolerant species begin to take over the forest. Ponderosa pine bark up to three inches thick is fire resistant and fire scars are very common on the trees. However the fires the pine can withstand must be fast moving and cooler than fires in heavy litter. Recent fire suppression practices have contributed to hotter, more damaging fires. As a Forest Service road surveyor during the summers in my college years, I was called to a fire that started to crown in the trees and watched as the pines literally exploded like a huge match being lit. Today the remaining mature groves are being managed more intelligently by the use of controlled burns where necessary.

Ponderosa pines eventually succumb to bark beetles, lightning strikes, or hot fires, but they can still stand a century or two as a barkless skeleton, dead on the inside. Even in death the trees provide homes for beetles, ants, fungi, lichens, and birds.

There is nothing like the sigh of the wind blowing through the crowns of a large tree. I often recall my time in the Forest Service, having lunch under a large ponderosa pine while being serenaded by the breeze flowing through the high needles and cones.

72. Purple Sage

Zane Grey's bestselling novel *Riders of the Purple Sage* is credited with establishing the western genre in literature. Published in 1912, it is a story of persecution and love that ends with the hero and heroine and their adopted child finding a paradise valley in the arid mountains of Utah. To avoid pursuit, they topple a balanced rock into the only entrance in and out of the paradise valley. It is a tale of the hope and redemption to be found in the vacant spaces of the American West, and it spurred in me an interest in purple sage.

While there is some disagreement about which sage Zane Grey was referring to in his novel, *Salvia dorrii* is thought to be the sage in question. *Salvia dorrii* has conspicuous purple flowers and is used in Native American ceremonies as a mild hallucinogen. It is native to the West, including Utah.

Purple sage is a true sage (genus *Salvia*) and which is different from sagebrush (genus *Artemisia*). Purple sage has a strong, aromatic fragrance. Unlike big sagebrush it is allelopathic—its leaves produce terpenes that interfere with the germination and growth of grasses and other plants that try to grow near the sage and take water. Purple sage is a low, round shrub seldom more than two feet in height, and throughout the Great Basin it grows on dry slopes and rocky bluffs. Purple sage is pollinated by bees, and some species of *Salvia* are important in the production of honey (Mozingo 1987).

Purple sage is important in the romantic imagination of the American West. Three different western bands were named Riders of the Purple Sage and a rock band was named New Riders of the Purple Sage. A town in Wyoming is named Purple Sage. All were inspired by Zane Grey's novel and the plant itself.

73. Quaking Aspen

Aspen grove

THERE IS NOTHING COMPARABLE to aspen leaves fluttering in the wind with their distinctive music. With leaves that appear to tremble, the quaking aspen is well named. A deciduous tree widely distributed in North America, the aspen grows up to eighty-two feet tall in moist meadows or seeps at higher elevations in the Oregon steppe. The bark is smooth and white with black scars and knots. The leaves have flattened petioles that make them flexible and are glossy green but dull underneath, both of which contribute to the tree's flashing appearance.

The aspen has male and female catkins on different trees. The catkins are about 2 inches long. Seeds are wind-dispersed in a cottony fluff. Because their seeds have no protective coating or food source, aspen are not successful at reproducing by seed dispersal. Instead, the tree propagates primarily from root sprouts forming extensive colonies of clones sharing a single root structure. Groves from a single root colony often turn color earlier or later or turn a slightly different color than neighboring colonies.

The colony of clones is considered to be a single organism. A colony named Pando in Utah is considered to be 80,000 years old, although some scientists believe that it may be as much as a million years old. Pando covers 106 acres and has 47,000 individual stems or trees, some of which are 130 years old.

Arborglyphs on quaking aspen

Aspen grow fast and are used for pulp to make paper and other products. Pioneers and Native Americans used the bark medicinally as a quinine substitute.

The aspen groves in the Steens Mountains and the Warner Mountains often contain arborglyphs or bark carvings. Basque sheepherders from the Pyrenees of France and Spain left carvings of names, dates, and even poetry in aspens on Steens Mountain. In Lake County and the Warner Mountains, the sheepherder-arborglyph makers were more likely to be Irish immigrants. The Basques left more aspen tree carvings than any other group. When surveying forest roads for the Forest Service, I encountered many arborglyphs. Later while hunting for petroglyphs in the Oregon desert, it was not unusual to find aspen tree carvings, some very old and faded. At Colvin Lake, for instance, are aspen groves that were once sheepherder camps. Some of the rocks near the lake are marked with petroglyphs. Here, both ancient, native people, and in more recent history, sheepherders, have left records of their presence.

One of my most sacred places on the earth is an aspen grove up Deep Creek canyon west of Adel, Oregon. The grove was one of our favorite camping spots as we sought the redband trout with rod and fly. The grove had a constantly flowing ice-cold spring of pure water that, when we drank from it, never failed to make us feel connected to the earth.

74. Steens Mountain Thistle Steens Mountain Paintbrush

Steens Mountain thistle

THE STEENS MOUNTAIN THISTLE, an endemic plant, has probably been isolated on the mountain since the Pleistocene. It grows on disturbed soils on the mountain or on stream banks and is common on the loop road above six thousand feet. It is also found in the nearby Pueblo Mountains. It is a perennial plant that grows two to four feet high. The flower is purple and appears all summer. The leaves are six to eight inches long with long yellow spines. Thistles can be a favorite source of nectar for several species of fritillary butterflies as well as goldfinches.

Steens Mountain thistle should not be confused with the noxious weed, Russian thistle, which was introduced to North America when seeds arrived in a contaminated shipment of flaxseed. The Russian thistle is famously known in Western folklore and songs as the tumbleweed. As it dries out and bounces along in the wind, it disperses thousands of seeds. (A single plant can disperse 200,000 seeds.) Russian thistle puts down very deep taproots, often in excess of ten feet, which enable it to thrive in arid and semi-arid regions of the West.

Steens Mountain paintbrush (*Castilleja pilosa*), like the thistle, is an endemic perennial restricted to slopes above 6,500 feet on Steens Mountain. Unlike most paintbrush, which are shades of red, the Steens Mountain paintbrush is a yellow-green color, similar to the rare green-tinged paintbrush found at Lost Forest. The genus is named after Domingo Castillejo, a Spanish botanist.

The flowers of Indian paintbrush are edible and were consumed by various Native American tribes. However they have a tendency to concentrate the toxic selenium and can be poisonous if not consumed properly in moderation.

It seems ironic that two of the rarest endemics on Steens Mountain are so different in their structure and makeup—one is a colorful plant without spines, and the other a spiny plant no one wants to touch.

75. Western Juniper

WESTERN JUNIPER is a common associate of sagebrush in Oregon's remote quarter. The foliage of this evergreen tree is very scaly with blue berries that look like they are covered in frost. (It is not wise to eat these berries.) Sometimes the bark is so gnarled, twisted, and barren that the tree appears to be dead. (In this regard it resembles the bristlecone pine.) Junipers grow on dry, rocky ground and do not form dense forest stands because of their solitary quest for water. Juniper is aromatic and the wood is very tough.

Juniper trees in the Oregon steppe can grow eighty to ninety feet in height. They compete with ponderosa pines for water and sunlight. In the Lost Forest both species are found, although the pine far outnumbers the juniper. The Lost Forest boasts what is probably the largest and oldest juniper in Oregon, measuring seventy-eight feet tall and six feet in diameter, and estimated to be two to four hundred years old. (A juniper in California is over eighty-five feet tall and fourteen feet in diameter and is estimated to be up to 3,000 years old [Lanner 1983].)

Juniper cones are a food source for several birds including robins and cedar waxwing. These birds digest the cone scales and disperse the seeds in their droppings. About half of junipers have both sexes on the same plant while the other half of the trees have cones of only one sex.

The Juniper trees name *Juniperus occidentalis* is derived from the Latin word *juniperus*. In Latin, *juniperus* is combination of the word *junio,* which means young, and *parere,* to produce. These aromatic, rugged, and durable trees are well-suited to the Oregon steppe.

76. Yellow Rabbitbrush

Rabbitbrush at Lake Abert

Two species of rabbitbrush are found in the Oregon steppe: *Chrysothamnus viscidiflorus*, yellow rabbitbrush (sometimes called green rabbitbrush); and *Ericameria nauseosa*, rubber rabbitbrush. The yellow rabbitbrush grows up to three feet tall while the rubber rabbitbrush can grow two to seven feet tall.

Rabbitbrush is tolerant of coarse, well-drained, and alkaline soils. It grows well on saline soils rich in calcium, and on disturbed areas such as roadsides and mined land. It is a browse for livestock and larger animals such as deer, elk, and antelope. It also provides cover for sage grouse, small birds, and rodents as well as forage for certain species of butterflies. Rabbitbrush associates with big sagebrush and ponderosa pine.

Rabbitbrush was used by native peoples for chewing gum, dye, and to treat colds. During World Wars I and II, rubber rabbitbrush was used to manufacture a rubber substitute. Rubber rabbitbrush growing near Los Alamos, New Mexico, has been found to concentrate strontium-90—a radioactive fission product—up to 300,000 times. Because of this, the rabbitbrush was considered as a plant to clean radioactive contamination from soils, wherein the brush could be harvested and the radioactivity removed from the soil.

On the Oregon steppe in late summer and fall, the widespread, vivid yellow rabbitbrush dominates the sage and alkali flats where it grows in great abundance.

Appendices

I. Timeline for Selected Places

The places featured in this book range from the Steens Mountain basalt lava flows dating back 16 million years to the early ranching era of the late 1800s and early 1900s and the sawmilling era of the 1940s and 1950s. The Pleistocene era from 12 million to 12,000 years ago is important in the geologic history of many of these places because of the deep glacial pluvial lakes and their subsequent drying beginning in the late Pleistocene. The late Pleistocene was also important in the cultural history of the region, including the Chewaucan culture described in the chapter on Lake Abert.

Following is a list of featured places, their chapters in the book (which correspond with their numbers on the map), and the time period or periods they best represent.

1. The Round Barn—Constructed late 1870s to early 1880s.
2. Diamond Craters—Late Pleistocene to recent eruptions.
3. Steens Mountain—Basalt flows from 16 million years ago. Glaciated in Pleistocene.
4. Malheur National Wildlife Refuge—Established in 1908.
5. Malheur Cave—Late Pleistocene lava tube.
6. Borax Lake, Tum Tum Lake—Hydrothermal deposits on lake sediments of Lake Alvord, BP 3725 to 3655.
7. Shirk Ranch—1883–1914
8. Long Lake—Petroglyphs dating from near present to 6,600 (or more) years ago.
9. Greaser Petroglyph—Petroglyphs made from 12,000 to 7,500 years ago.
10. Stone Corral—Constructed late 1800s to early 1900s.
11. Stone Bridge—Constructed 1867.
12. Sunstones—Formed in Steens Mountain flows up to 16 million years ago.

13. Petroglyph Lake—Petroglyphs dating from thousands to hundreds of years BP.
14. Lake Abert—Part of pluvial lake Chewaucan, began drying in late Pleistocene.
15. Alkali Lake—Began drying in late Pleistocene.
16. Willow Ranch—Active 1930–1959.
17. Lily Lake—Formed by glaciation in Pleistocene.
18. Dog Lake—Campground established in 1934.
19. Chewaucan River—Pleistocene era to present.
20. Gearhart Mountain—Formed six to eight million years ago.
21. Sycan Marsh—Restoration began 1980.
22. Cottonwood Meadows—Formed by earthen dam constructed in 1961.
23. Summer Lake and Hot Springs—Remnant of pluvial Lake Chewaucan, named by John C. Fremont in 1843.
24. Slide Lakes—Formed by late Pleistocene landslides.
25. Fort Rock—Tuff ring formed fifty to one hundred thousand years ago.
26. Lost Forest—3,200 years ago to present.
27. Glass Buttes—Volcanic complex erupted about 5.5 million years ago.

II. Proposed Trip Plan

There a number of ways to see the places listed in Part One. On the following page is a proposed trip plan that begins and ends in Burns, Oregon, and flows in a clockwise direction. Gas, food, and lodging are scarce on this route, so those who are not wilderness campers or are self-contained with a camper or RV will want to establish base camps from which they can make side trips. There are large portions of the Oregon Outback where one can pitch a tent or park a camper just about anywhere. Some of the campgrounds offered by the state and the Forest Service are marked on the map. One or more campgrounds are also available on the Steens Mountain Loop, Hart Mountain Antelope Refuge, and Summer Lake Refuge. These are mentioned in the specific chapters relating to these places.

I prefer staying in a location with food and lodging available and taking side trips. This approach tends to maximize the time that can be spent exploring and even though there is some backtracking required, there are always interesting things to see along the way.

Proposed trip plan—a circle beginning and ending in Burns, Oregon, with suggested stops along the way.		
Stop	**Places to see**	**Recommended facilities**
1-Burns, OR	Begin trip here.	Best Western in Hines. Gas stations and restaurants available.
2-Diamond or Frenchglen, OR	• Round Barn • Diamond Craters • Steens Mountain • Malheur Refuge • Malheur Cave	Hotel Diamond or Frenchglen Hotel. Both historic hotels with family style meals. Gas available at Frenchglen.
3-Fields, OR	• Borax Lake • Tum Tum Lake	Lodging (Alvord Inn), food and gas available.
4-Plush, OR	• Shirk Ranch • Greaser Petroglyph • Stone Corral and Warner Lakes • Stone Bridge • Sunstone collection site • Petroglyph Lake • Long Lake	Rental cabin available at Plush (Hart Mountain Cabin). Groceries and gas available at Plush store.
5-Lakeview, OR	• Willow Ranch • Lily Lake and High Grade mines • Lake Abert • Alkali Lake • Dog Lake • Cottonwood Meadows	Lodging (Fremont Inn or Best Western), restaurants, and gas available.
6-Summer Lake Hot Springs, OR	• Chewaucan River • Summer Lake Refuge • Slide Lakes • Gearhart Mountain • Sycan Marsh	Rental cabins (Summer Lake Hot Springs Resort). Food and gas available in Paisley, OR.
7-Christmas Valley, OR	• Fort Rock • Lost Forest • Glass Buttes (on route to Burns)	Lodging, gas, and food available in Christmas Valley (Christmas Valley Desert Inn).
8-Burns, OR	End of trip	

III. Trip Hazards and Vehicle Recommendations

Trip Hazards and Precautions

- **Rattlesnakes**—Rattlesnakes will try to avoid you and it is best to let them. Wear long pants and boots. Use caution when reaching down near rocks or brushy areas. Rattlesnakes may not rattle in the spring or when shedding their skin.
- **Lack of water**—Much of the Oregon Outback is arid or semi-arid. Take plenty of water.
- **Mosquitoes**—In some places mosquitoes can be a real problem. Take repellent.
- **Ticks**—Ticks are troublesome particularly in the spring and early summer. It is best to do a thorough inspection of the body and clothing when coming in from the field. Tick repellents are also available.
- **Gas**—Gas stations are few and very far between. It is best to top off the tank at every opportunity or to carry a spare can.
- **Heat and sun**—In the summer the desert can get very hot. Because of the high elevation the sun is particularly hard on the skin. It is best to wear a good hat to shade the face and to use sun block on exposed body parts.
- **Getting lost**—This is not as much of an issue as it used to be thanks to GPS technology. It is still advisable to take good maps. These are available at the Forest Service and BLM offices. See page 152.
- **Lack of communication**—Cell phone service is problematic and may not be available at all in large parts of the backcountry.
- **Extreme weather**—The desert gets very cold at night even in the summer. Thunderstorms, hail, and downpours are frequent in the summer. Sudden high wind gusts can occur even in clear, sunny weather. It is possible to encounter snow in the summer at the higher elevations. A good rule of thumb is to be prepared for any weather at any time.

Vehicle Recommendations by Site

Listed sites are accessible to passenger vehicles with exceptions and precautions noted.

- **Alkali Lake**. Accessible from Highway 395. Be aware of hazardous waste site at southeast corner of lake.
- **Borax Lake and Tum Tum Lake**. Road to Borax Lake is not paved but passable. Tum Tum Lake is accessible from paved Highway 205.
- **Chewaucan River**. Good road from Paisley up to campgrounds in canyon.
- **Cottonwood Meadows**. No extraordinary hazards.
- **Diamond Craters**. Beware of sharp rocks in roads.
- **Dog Lake**. No extraordinary hazards.
- **Fort Rock**. Accessible from paved roads.
- **Gearhart Mountain**. Good forest service roads, though narrow in places. Be aware of logging trucks and cattle on road.
- **Glass Buttes**. Roads may have sharp rocks.
- **Greaser Petroglyph**. Good road from Highway 140 junction.
- **Lake Abert**. Lake is accessible via Highway 395. Use turnouts because traffic can be dangerous.
- **Lily Lake and High Grade Mines**. Road is very steep and narrow in places. Not suitable for trailers or campers. Passenger cars use caution.
- **Long Lake**. Very rough, slow, and rocky road from Highway 140 junction. Very isolated area with no cell phone service. Take spare water cans. Be prepared for wilderness camping. High clearance, ten-ply tires, and full-size spare tires essential.
- **Lost Forest**. Very isolated. Road is deeply gullied in places. High clearance vehicle required.
- **Malheur Refuge**. Main road through pond areas can be very rough and washboarded.
- **Malheur Cave**. Short distance from paved Highway 78.

- **Petroglyph Lake**. Road to lake is problematic from junction with the Hart Mountain Refuge headquarters road. High clearance vehicle is recommended. Washboard roads throughout the refuge.
- **Round Barn**. Improved roads all the way.
- **Shirk Ranch**. Road is dirt and unimproved from Highway 140 junction so progress can be slow and dusty. Passenger car okay, but SUV recommended.
- **Slide Lakes**. Steep forest service road with switchbacks. Drive slowly.
- **Steens Mountain**. South part of loop road is steep and rocky in places and requires high clearance. Strong, ten-ply tires are recommended.
- **Stone Bridge**. Road is muddy and getting mired a real possibility in spring. Road is rough in places. Four-wheel drive recommended and high clearance helpful.
- **Stone Corral and Warner Lakes**. Four-wheel drive and high clearance recommended. Road north of Hart Mountain Refuge headquarters junction can be problematic in spring. Getting mired in mud a real hazard.
- **Summer Lake Hot Springs and Summer Lake Refuge**. Accessible from Highway 31. No extraordinary hazards. Refuge has good road network through pond areas. Car can be used as a blind for spotting wildlife.
- **Sunstone Collection Site**. Road can be washboarded and dusty. Passenger car okay, but SUV preferable.
- **Sycan Marsh**. May encounter washboard roads.
- **Willow Ranch and Goose Lake**. Accessible from Highway 395. No extraordinary hazards.

IV. Selected Side Trips

If you visit **Steens Mountain**, also see:

- Mann Lake. A prized fishing lake on the east side of the Steens Mountain escarpment, noted for Lahontan cutthroat trout.

If you visit **Hart Mountain National Antelope Refuge**, also see:

- DeGarmo Canyon. This steep-sided canyon on the west-facing escarpment of Hart Mountain features waterfalls and spring flowers, and is a prized location for rock hounds.

If you visit **Warner Mountain**, also see:

- Colvin Lake and Timbers. There are petroglyphs around the lake, as well as an aspen grove that was a sheepherders camp, with carvings on the aspen trees. Colvin Timbers is an anomalous ponderosa pine forest. Both are east of Abert Rim, four miles north of the northern boundary of Fremont National Forest in the Warner Mountains. Take Forest Road 3615 until it ends at the boundary. The road is maintained to the boundary, but the last four miles is an unmaintained jeep trail.

If you visit **Christmas Valley**, also see:

- Christmas Valley Air Force Station. An over-the-horizon radar station made obsolete by the end of the Cold War featuring an impressive antenna array. East of Christmas Valley.

- Fossil Lake. A notable fossil location near the Lost Forest.

- Fort Rock Homestead Village Museum. Features structures and artifacts from the homesteading era. Near Fort Rock and Christmas Valley. www.fortrockoregon.com/frvhs.html

- Crack-in-the-Ground. A large volcanic fissure over two miles long and up to seventy feet deep.

V. Children's Checklist

When travelling with my grandson in the Oregon outback, I have found that a good experience for him is to keep a notebook and sketchbook to record the things that he can find and see along the way. I provided him with a set of colored pencils and an artist pad for this endeavor. His list, like the one below, contained thirty items and he was able to find and learn about all but three of them. He was rewarded with an engraved rock hammer in honor of his accomplishment.

X	Item
	Agate
	Alkali saltgrass
	Basalt
	California quail
	Cottontail or jackrabbit
	Coyote
	Desert varnish
	Dust devil
	Halophyte and xerophyte
	Jasper
	Killdeer
	Lenticular clouds
	Microbiotic crust
	Porcupine
	Petrified wood
	Petroglyph

	Pluvial lake
	Ponderosa pine
	Pronghorn antelope
	Purple sage
	Quaking aspen
	Red-winged blackbird
	Sagebrush
	Steens Mountain thistle and paintbrush
	Thunder egg
	Vernal pool
	Virga
	Western juniper
	White pelican
	Yellow rabbitbrush

VI. Information Resources

Bend, Oregon

High Desert Museum
59800 S. Highway 97
Bend, OR 97702
541-382-4754
www.highdesertmuseum.org

Permanent outdoor exhibits include the Miller Family Ranch, Lazinka Sawmill, birds of prey, otter, bobcat, and a nature walk. An indoor, walk-through exhibit focuses on Oregon's Native American, exploration, trapping, pioneer, and mining history. Museum has a bookstore with titles on eastern Oregon.

Burns, Oregon

Harney County Historical Museum
18 West D Street
Burns, Oregon 97720
541-573-5618
www.hchistoricalsociety.com

Photographs, local bird collection, Native American artifacts, and a pioneer kitchen.

Highland Rock and Gem
1316 Hines Blvd.
Burns, Oregon
541-573-5119

A good resource for rock hounds.

John Day, Oregon

Kam Wah Chung State Heritage Site
125 NW Canton
John Day, OR 97845
oregonstateparks.org/index.cfm?do=parkPage.
dsp_parkPage&parkId=5

This original apothecary and store built in 1870 by Chinese immigrants Lung On and Doc Hay highlights Chinese culture in eastern Oregon. Doc Hay's herbal medicine practice served Chinese and European-American patients throughout the region.

Lakeview, Oregon

Lake County Museum
118 South E Street
Lakeview, OR 97630
541-947-2220
www.lakecountyor.org/links/museum.php

Along with the Schminck Memorial Museum, located just a few doors down at 128 South E Street, the Lake County Museum focuses on Native American and pioneer history and artifacts.

U.S. Bureau of Land Management (BLM)
Regional Office-Lakeview
1301 S. "G" Street
Lakeview, OR 97630
541-947-2177
www.blm.gov/or/districts/lakeview

The BLM provides information, including maps and brochures, about the extensive lands they administer in the remote quarter.

Fremont-Winema National Forest Headquarters
1301 South G Street
Lakeview, OR 97630
541-947-2151
www.fs.usda.gov/fremont-winema

Information and maps covering the extensive Fremont National Forest. Ranger stations also have information at Bly, Paisley, and Silver Lake.

Hart Mountain National Antelope Refuge Main Office
20995 Rabbit Hill Road, PO Box 111
Lakeview, Oregon 97630
541-947-3315
www.fws.gov/refuge/Hart_Mountain

The office is in Lakeview, but refuge headquarters are east of Plush-Hart Mountain Road.

Established in 1936 to protect habitat of the American pronghorn antelope (*Antilocapra americana*) and other species.

Madras, Oregon

Richardsons Rock Ranch
6683 NE Haycreek Rd
Madras, OR 97741
541-475-2680
richardsonrockranch.com

A must-visit for any rock hound, the ranch—which includes the Priday Agate beds—is a major source of thunder eggs and for a small fee, visitors can dig their own and have them cut at the shop. The ranch has a vast collection of rocks from eastern Oregon as well as worldwide including fossils. The ranch is northeast of Madras, Oregon, off Highway 97. The junction to the ranch is well marked.

Malheur National Wildlife Refuge

Headquarters
36391 Sodhouse Lane
Princeton, Oregon 97721
541-493-2612
www.fws.gov/refuge/Malheur

Features viewing ponds, a bookshop, displays, and a museum with a good collection of mounted birds and animals found on the refuge. Near the refuge off Lava Bed Road is the Pete French Round Barn, a remnant of the P Ranch cattle empire. A private group has built a visitor center, museum, gift shop, and bookstore near the barn.

Portland, Oregon

Oregon Department of Geology and Mineral Industries
800 NE Oregon Street, Suite 965
Portland, Oregon 97232-2162
971-673-1555
www.oregongeology.org

The Oregon Department of Geology and Mineral Industries (DOGAMI) website offers a huge selection of books, maps, and field guides to help plan your trip.

Essential Brochures and Maps

The following maps and brochures are available from the sources listed above.

John Day, Oregon, area

- Kam Wah Chung State Heritage Site brochure
- Strawberry Mountain Wilderness map and brochure—U.S. Forest Service

Fremont National Forest area

- Gearhart Mountain Wilderness map—Fremont National Forest
- Fremont National Forest map—U.S. Forest Service

Steens Mountain area

- Malheur National Wildlife Refuge brochure and map—Refuge or U.S. Fish and Wildlife Service
- Diamond Craters: Oregon's Geologic Gem—BLM
- Steens High Desert Country—Pacific Northwest Recreation Map Series—BLM
- Steens Mountain Recreation Lands Oregon brochure—BLM

Adel, Oregon, high desert area

- Surface Management Status map, Adel, Oregon—topographic map—BLM

VII. Place Names in the Remote Quarter

Adel. The small town in Warner Valley was allegedly named by an early settler, Mrs. Jacob Messner, after a favorite local cow named Leda, spelled backwards.

Alvord Lake. This alkali (playa) lake was named by George Currey of the First Oregon Cavalry in honor of General Benjamin Alvord of the U.S. Army. Alvord Lake is at the foot of the east escarpment of the Steens Mountain.

Beaty's Butte. This butte was named by Colonel C. S. Drew of the Owyhee Reconnaissance with the 1st Oregon Cavalry in 1864 in honor of Sergeant A. M. Beaty.

Bly. This small town in Lake County is named from a Klamath Indian word meaning "up" or "high."

Burns. This community was named for the Scottish poet Robert Burns by local resident Archie McGowan.

Chewaucan Marsh. This marsh is fed by the Chewaucan River, which drains into Lake Abert. The name derives from the Klamath Indian word *tchua* meaning wild potato and *keni* meaning place.

Crane Creek. This creek flows from the west side of the Warner Mountains into Goose Lake. The creek was named after Samuel Crane who settled on the creek in 1869.

Gearhart Mountain. The mountain is named after James Gearhart and his brother William. They were in the cattle business in the area.

Goose Lake. Goose Lake was probably named during pioneer days because of the large number of migrating wild geese that stopped at the lake on the Pacific Flyway. Explorer John Work of the Hudson's Bay Company mentioned "Pit Lake" in his journal of his exploration of the area. Pit Lake probably referred to the animal trap pits made by the Achomawi tribe who lived near the lake. Pit Lake was later named Goose Lake by the pioneers who came to its shore after crossing the Warner Mountains on the Applegate trail. The settlers then split with some going south to the California gold fields and others going on to the Willamette Valley.

Guano Lake. This playa lake east of Hart Mountain was named by the Owyhee Reconnaissance under Colonel C. S. Drew in 1864. It was named for the guano deposits along the banks of the lake.

Harney Lake. Harney Lake was named by Captain H. D. Wallen of the Fourth Infantry in honor of General W. S. Harney of the Department of Oregon.

Hart Mountain. The name came from a ranch brand that used a heart as a symbol. The vaqueros did not know the correct spelling and named the mountain after their brand.

Lake Abert. Explorer John Work of the Hudson's Bay Company named the lake Salt Lake. Later John Fremont on his expedition named the lake after Colonel J. J. Abert of the U.S. Topographical Engineers.

Lakeview. This town was named by the citizens in 1876. Goose Lake was larger at that time and very close to the town. In May 1900 every business in town burned to the ground but reconstruction was completed by fall.

Malheur Lake. Peter Skene Ogden's party came upon the lake in 1826. It was named after the Malheur River, meaning "unfortunate river" in French. It was a freshwater lake separated from salty Harney Lake by a natural dike.

New Pine Creek. This small town is said to be the oldest in Oregon. It was intended to be named after the nearby Pine Creek but postal authorities objected so it was named New Pine Creek. Pine Creek is located directly on the Oregon/California border.

Paisley. This small town on the Chewaucan River was named by a Scottish pioneer after a place of that name in Scotland.

Plush. Folklore has it that this small village near Hart Mountain was named when an Indian was playing poker with some cowboys. The Indian allegedly put down his hand and said "plush" instead of flush.

Quartz Mountain. This mountain is named after a prominent ledge of quartz about thirty miles west of Lakeview.

Silver Lake. It is not known who gave this lake its descriptive name. On Christmas Eve of 1894 a fire at a community party killed forty-three people. Ed O'Farrel rode one hundred miles over poor or nonexistent roads in the dead of winter to fetch Dr. Daly in Lakeview. Daly rode twenty-four hours in his buggy to reach Silver Lake. The O'Farrell ride is noted as one of the most historic rides in the history of the American West. A monument at Silver Lake honors the people who died in the fire.

Summer Lake. This sixty-square-mile playa lake at the foot of Winter Ridge escarpment was named by John C. Fremont, during his expedition of the U.S. Topographical Engineers in December 1843. The lake is supplied by a spring-fed stream named Ana River.

Sycan Marsh. The marsh gets its name from the Klamath Indian words *saiga* and *keni* that means level, grassy place. Its outlet, the Sycan River, is a tributary of the Sprague River. The marsh was once a part of the vast ZX ranch but the marsh was sold to the Nature Conservancy for restoration as fish and bird habitat. However some compatible ranching still occurs at the marsh. The Sycan River is designated a national Wild and Scenic River.

VIII. Glossary

Aeolian. Geologic features as a result of the action of the wind (e.g. sand dunes).

Alkaline. Having a pH of 7 or greater, as opposed to an acid. A number of the lakes in the remote quarter are alkaline or were alkaline and have left behind alkali flats.

Alluvial. Geologic features as a result of the action of water (e.g. sediment deposits).

Arboglyph. A carving typically made on a quaking aspen tree. In the Great Basin these were usually made by Basque and Irish sheepherders in the aspen groves where they camped.

Caldera. A volcanic crater typically caused by a volcanic eruption followed by a collapse.

Caliche. A layer of calcium carbonate formed in a soil. Caliche layers are barriers to water infiltration. Caliche layers are responsible in part for anomalous ponderosa pine forests at the Lost Forest and Colvin Timbers.

Cinder cone. A cone formed during a volcanic eruption by materials thrown out of the volcano. Cinder cones are made of glassy, pyroclastic materials containing gas bubbles frozen in place that cooled quickly when exposed to the air.

Cirque. A steep-sided semi-circular bowl formed at the head of a glacier by glacial action. Look for these at Steens Mountain, Warner Mountain, and Gearhart Mountain.

Conchoidal fractures. Concentric, semi-circular fractures in a glassy material such as obsidian.

Endemic. A plant or animal found only in a certain place—a native plant or animal. A number of endemics are found in the remote quarter particularly on isolated mountain ranges like Steens Mountain and Hart Mountain.

Eutrophication. A process that fills a lake or pond with excessive organic material and sediments over time due to an abundance of nutrients. Eventually the water body fills to become a meadow and then a forest. Look for this process in the lakes and ponds of Steens Mountain.

Fault block. Very large blocks of rock formed by stresses and movement in the earth's crust. When blocks slide horizontally, a strike-slip fault results. If the displacement is vertical an escarpment or steep slope forms on one side of the block and a gentler slope on the other side (e.g. Steens Mountain).

Halophyte. A plant that has adapted to growing in saline (salty) conditions (see Chapters 42, 45, and 46).

Horst and graben. In a normal, vertical fault, a block that is pushed upward is a horst and a block that has dropped due to faulting is a graben. In the remote quarter there are a number of examples of horst and graben topography including Steens Mountain, Hart Mountain, the Warner Mountains, and Winter Ridge and Summer Lake. For instance, Abert Rim is an example of a horst while Abert Lake has accumulated in the graben next to the rim.

Krummholz. Stunted trees due to wind action exposed near the tree line and summits of ranges in the remote quarter.

Lacustrine. Associated with lakes.

Lava Tube. A natural tunnel formed within a lava flow wherein the top of the flow solidified while the lava beneath flowed out, leaving a long void or cave (e.g. Malheur Cave).

Maar. A volcanic crater formed by explosive action when lava comes into contact with groundwater. A small maar can be found at Diamond Craters. Hole-in-the-Ground in Lake County is a large maar. There are at least forty maars in the remote quarter with many remaining unnamed.

Macrophyte. An aquatic plant large enough to be seen by the eye. Eutrophic lakes have large populations of macrophytes.

Magadite. A hydrous sodium silicate mineral formed by precipitation from evaporating alkaline brines. This mineral can be found at Alkali Lake.

Microbiotic crust. Arid-land soil crusts formed of a consolidated combination of cyanobacteria, eukaryotic algae, fungi, lichens, and bryophytes. Also known as cryptogams (see Chapter 47).

Moraine. A mass of soil and rock deposited at the foot of a glacier. Look for these at Steens Mountain. Lily Lake in the Warner Mountains is dammed by a moraine.

Omnivorous. An animal able to eat both plant and animal foods.

Petroglyph. A rock carving made by Native peoples by scrapping through the desert varnish (see Chapter 43) on rocks to leave a picture or symbol. See the Long Lake, Petroglyph Lake, Stone Bridge, and the Greaser Petroglyph site.

Pictograph. A rock painting made by Native peoples. Often found at petroglyph sites, but more rare. Paints were made from natural minerals and mixed with water, blood, urine, or egg yolk. Excellent examples can be found at the Stone Bridge site (see Chapter 11).

Pioneer plant. A species that can colonize a difficult environment to begin the process of soil formation. A prime example in the remote quarter is the lichen.

Playa. A flat, dry basin formed from a drying lake. In the remote quarter many playa lakes are remnants of large, deep lakes from the Pleistocene era. A good example is the Alvord Desert at the eastern foot of the Steens Mountain escarpment.

Pyroclastic. Rocks or fragments of rocks ejected from an exploding volcano.

Riparian. The zone next to a river or stream bank. These areas are of critical importance to the ecology of the remote quarter.

Saline. A solution of salt in water, or soils containing high levels of salt. Highly saline lakes and soils are common in the remote quarter (e.g. Lake Abert).

Shiller. An optical effect in a mineral wherein the interior flickers when held to the light due to inclusions of reflecting elements or minerals. An excellent example is the sunstone (see Chapter 12).

Steppe. A large area of grassland. The remote quarter is largely a semi-arid steppe.

Symbiotic. An association of two or more animals or plants for mutual advantage. The lichen is an example of a symbiosis between algae and fungi.

Tarn. A lake occupying a cirque of glacial origin. Look for these on Steens Mountain, Gearhart Mountain, and the Warner Mountains.

Thermal. A rising spiraling column of air caused by convection of warm air. Thermals can become visible when carrying dust (dust devil) or salt or when flocks of birds, such as white pelicans, circle in them to gain lift.

Tuff. Tuff is a mixture of volcanic rock and mineral fragments in a volcanic ash matrix often formed when magma contacts groundwater, resulting in an explosive event (see maar). Fort Rock is an example of a tuff ring (see Chapter 25).

Wigwam burner. A conical metal structure used by sawmills to burn scrap wood and sawdust in a controlled manner. These structures are often the last artifact remaining at the sawmill sites throughout the West. They are no longer used, for economic and environmental reasons.

Xerophyte. A plant that can grow with little water (see Chapter 45).

Warner Mountain corral and meadow

Quantum

A discrete amount of light, energy or charge in nature.

Standing on the bluff
of the flaming autumn
with red and orange
dancing below
in the grassy wind
of the ice blue day
stabbed
by the shafts of
the sun burning hills amid
the cold sloshing ponds
darting birds, circling birds
in swirling columns of
invisible air
crying
salty marsh tears
not wanting to leave
but being called by
far off cranes.

Lord let me come back
here if only a mote of
dust, a mole of wind,
a quantum of light,
let me crawl in the grass
and be a feast for a red tail
or speared by an egret
even the howl of a coyote
would be enough for me
in this golden mystery,
this sacred ground,
this all.

References and Additional Reading

Adams, Melvin R. 2001. *Netting the Sun: A Personal Geography of the Oregon Desert*. Pullman: Washington State University Press.

______. 2002. "Petroglyphs of the Oregon High Desert." *Shamanism and Myth: World Journal of Prehistoric and Primitive Art* 33. Valcominica, Italy: Centro Camuno Di Studi Preistorici.

Allen, Barbara. 1987. *Homesteading the High Desert*. Salt Lake City: University of Utah Press.

Allison, Ira S. 1979. *Pluvial Fort Rock Lake, Lake County, Oregon*. Portland: State of Oregon Department of Geology and Mineral Industries.

______. 1982. *Geology of Pluvial Lake Chewaucan*. Corvallis: Oregon State University Press.

Arno, Stephen F. and Ramona P. Hammerly. 2007. *Northwest Trees*. Seattle: The Mountaineers.

Badger, Thomas and Robert Watters. 2002. "Seismogenic Landslide Modification of Fault Scarps, Summer Lake Basin, Lake County, Oregon." Geological Society of America, Cordilleran Section 98th Annual Meeting.

Barry, Pat. 1980. "Ferry Boat in the Desert: The Lovely Little *Lakeview*." *The Journal of the Modoc County Historical Society* 2.

Bates, Robert L. and Julia A. Jackson. 1957. *Dictionary of Geological Terms–Third Edition*. New York: American Geological Institute.

Bedwell, Stephen F. 1973. *Fort Rock Basin, Prehistory and Environment*. Eugene: University of Oregon Books.

Benedict, Ellen. 1985. "Diamond Craters. Oregon's Geologic Gem." Self-guided tour brochure. Bureau of Land Management, Hines, Oregon.

Brown, Rick. 2000. *Steens Mountain–Alvord Basin Objects of Historic and Scientific Interest*. Washington, DC: The Wilderness Society.

Christiansen, Kenneth and Peter Bellinger. 1996. "Cave *Pseudosinella* and *Oncopudura*, New to Science." *Journal of Cave and Karst Studies* 58 (1): 38-53.

Clark, Lewis J. 1998. *Wildflowers of the Pacific Northwest*. Madeira Park, BC: Harbour Publishing.

Cressman, Luther S. 1937. *Petroglyphs of Oregon*. Eugene: University of Oregon.

______. 1981. *The Sandal and the Cave*. Corvallis: Oregon State University Press.

Crook, George. 1960. *General George Crook: His Autobiography*. Norman: University of Oklahoma Press.

Cummings, Michael L., Sean D. Wilson, and Anna M. St. John. 2010. "Borax Lake, a Thermal Lake Confined within a Biomorphic Mound, Pueblo Valley, Oregon." *Geofacets* 204.

Daehnke, Jon and Anan Raymond. 2008. *The Archaeology of Petroglyph Lake*. Cultural Resource Series 14. Portland: U.S. Fish and Wildlife Service.

Dorn, Ronald I. and T. M. Oberlander. 1981. "Microbial Origin of Desert Varnish." *Science* 213.

Eastman, Donald C. 1990. *Rare and Endangered Plants of Oregon*. Wilsonville, OR: Beautiful America Publishing Co.

Elftman, Herbert O. 1931. *Pleistocene Mammals of Fossil Lake, Oregon*. New York: American Museum of Natural History.

Eliade, Mercia. 2004. *Shamanism: Archaic Techniques of Ecstasy*. 2004. Princeton, NJ: Princeton University Press.

Flint, Richard F. 1957. *Glacial and Pleistocene Geology*. New York: John Wiley and Sons.

Fremont, John C. 1845. *Report of the Exploring Expedition to the Rocky Mountains in the Year 1842 and to Oregon and Northern California in the Years 1843-44*. Washington, DC: Gales and Seaton, Printers.

French, Giles. 1965. *Cattle Country of Peter French*. New York: Binfords and Mort.

Furnish, Joseph, James McIver, and Mark Teiser. 2002. "Algae and Invertebrates of a Great Basin Desert Hot Lake: A Description of the Borax Lake Ecosystem of Southeastern Oregon." *Conference Proceedings: Spring Fed Wetlands*. LaGrande, OR: USDA Forest Service, Pacific Northwest Research Station.

Gamma, Hans. 2011. *Picture Jaspers*. Fountain Hills, AZ: Self-published.

Geitgey, Ron. 1987. "Oregon Sunstones." *Oregon Geology*. Portland: Oregon Department of Geology and Mineral Industries. www.oregongeology.org/sub/learnmore/sunstones2.htm

Gillis, Julia. 1993. *So Far from Home*. Portland: Oregon Historical Society Press.

Hill, James M. 1915. *Some Mining Districts in Northeast California and Northwest Nevada*. Washington, DC: Government Printing Office.

Hill, Larry. 2000. "The End of the Line—Malheur Cave Survey." *National Speleological Society News* 58 (2).

Johnsgard, Paul A. 1991. *Crane Music: A Natural History of Cranes*. Lincoln: University of Nebraska Press.

Johnson, Daniel M. et al., eds. 1998. *Atlas of Oregon Lakes*. Corvallis: Oregon State University Press.

Johnson, Lars. 2014. *Rockhounding Oregon*. Helena, MT: Falcon Guides.

Kerst, Cary and Steve Gordon. 2011. *Dragonflies and Damselflies of Oregon*. Corvallis: Oregon State University Press.

Kniffen, Fred. 1928. *Achomawi Geography*. Berkeley: University of California Press.

Lanner, Ronald. 1983. *Trees of the Great Basin*. Reno: University of Nevada Press.

Larson, Ron. 2007. "Oregon Plants, Oregon Places: Gearhart Mountain Wilderness." *Kalmiopsis: Journal of the Native Plant Society of Oregon* 14. www.npsoregon.org/kalmiopsis/kalmiopsis14/larson.pdf.

Leopold, A. Starker. 1977. *The California Quail*. Berkeley: University of California Press.

Lewis, William and Paul Philips. 2006. *The Journal of John Work*. Norman: University of Oklahoma Press.

Lillie, Robert J. 2005. *Parks and Plates*. New York: W. W. Norton and Co.

Lockwood, John and Richard Hazlett. 2010. *Volcanoes: Global Perspectives*. Oxford, UK: John Wiley and Sons.

Loring, Malcolm and Louise Loring. 1996. *Pictographs and Petroglyphs of the Oregon Country*. Los Angeles: Institute of Archaeology, University of California.

Lukas, David. 1997. "Aspens." *Orion* 59.

______. 1999. *Watchable Birds of the Great Basin*. Missoula: Mountain Press Publishing Co.

MacLean, Norman. 1976. *A River Runs Through It*. Chicago: University of Chicago Press.

Mankinen, Michel et al. 1985. "The Steens Mountain (Oregon) Geomagnetic Polarity Transition." *Journal of Geophysical Research* 90 (B12).

Mansfield, Donald. 1995. "The Unique Botany of Steens Mountain: The Rare and Endemic Plants." *Kalmiopsis: Journal of the Native Plant Society of Oregon* 5.

Maugh, Thomas. 2012. "Who Was First? New Info on North America's Earliest Residents." *Los Angeles Times*, July 12.

McArthur, Lewis A. 1974. *Oregon Geographic Names*. Portland: Oregon Historical Society, 1974.

McMullen, Dean. 1994. *Oregon under Foot: Agate, Jasper, Opal, and Related Gems*. Portland: OMSI Press.

Mihalyo, Daniel. 1997. *Wood Burners*. New York: Princeton Architectural Press.

Mikesh, Robert C. 1978. *Japan's World War II Balloon Bomb Attacks on North America*. Smithsonian Annals of Flight 9. Washington, DC: Smithsonian Institution Press.

Miller, Jim 2013. "Obsidian is Hot Stuff." Oregon State University, Volcano World. volcano.oregonstate.edu/obsidian.

Minor, Rick, Stephen D. Beckham, and Kathryn A. Toepel. 1979. *Cultural Resource Overview of the BLM Lakeview District, South-Central Oregon: Archaeology, Ethnography, History*. University of Oregon Anthropological Papers 16. Eugene: University of Oregon Museum of Natural and Cultural History and Department of Anthropology.

Mozingo, Hugo N. 1987. *Shrubs of the Great Basin*. Reno: University of Nevada Press.

Myrick, David F. 1962. *Railroads of Nevada and Eastern California*. Berkeley, CA: Howell-North Books.

Neruda, Pablo and Ilan Stavans, ed. *The Poetry of Pablo Neruda*. 2003. New York: Farrar, Strauss, and Giroux.

Pabian, Roger. 2006. *Agates*. Buffalo, NY: Firefly Books.

Palmer, Kevin L. 1991. "The High Grade Mining District." *The Journal of the Modoc County Historical Society* 13. Warner Mountains Issue.

Palmer, Tim. 2014. *Field Guide to Oregon Rivers*. Corvallis: Oregon State University Press.

Peterson, Norman V. 1972. "Oregon Sunstones." *The Ore Bin* 32 (12).

Peterson, Norman V. and Edward A. Groh. 1964. "Diamond Craters, Oregon." *The Ore Bin* 26 (2).

Pettigrew, Richard. 1985. *Archaeological Investigations on the East Shore of Lake Abert, Lake County Oregon*. University of Oregon Anthropological Papers 32. Eugene: University of Oregon Museum of Natural and Cultural History and Department of Anthropology.

Phillips, Kenneth N. and A. S. Van Denburgh. 1985. *Hydrogeology and Geochemistry of Abert, Summer and Other Closed-Basin Lakes in South-Central Oregon*. Geological Survey Professional Paper 502-B. Washington, DC: U.S. Government Printing Office.

Porter, Gladys. 1987. "The History of Willow Ranch." *The Journal of the Modoc County Historical Society*.

Purvis, William. 2000. *Lichens*. Washington, DC: Smithsonian Institution Press.

Romaine, Garret. 2008. *Gem Trails of Oregon*. Upland, CA: Gem Guides Book Co.

Rooney, Thomas P., Blair F. Jones, and James T. Neal. 1969. "Magadiite from Alkali Lake, Oregon." *The American Mineralogist* 54.

Ryser, Fred A. 1985. *Birds of the Great Basin*. Reno: University of Nevada Press.

Schaefer, Vincent and John Day. 1981. *A Field Guide to the Atmosphere*. Boston: Houghton Mifflin Company.

Scheerer, Paul D. 2011. *Foskett Spring Speckled Dace Investigations*. Corvallis: Oregon Department of Fish and Wildlife.

Shirk, David L. 1956. *The Cattle Drives of David Shirk*. Portland: Champoeg Press.

Stewart, John L. 1999. *Fremont's Greatest Western Exploration*. Vancouver, WA: Set, Inc.

Taylor, Ronald. 1992. *Sagebrush Country: A Wildflower Sanctuary*. Missoula, MT: Mountain Press Publishing Co.

Toomey, David. 2013. *Weird Life*. New York: W. W. Norton.

Turpin, Solveig, ed. 1994. *Shamanism and Rock Art in North America*. San Antonio: Rock Art Foundation.

Webber, Bert. 1993. *The Oregon and Applegate Trail Diary of Welborn Beeson in 1853*. Medford, OR: Webb Research Group.

Weisel, George F. and Eldon L. McLaury. 1964. "Blind Catfish (*Ictalurus nebulosus*) from Dog Lake, Oregon." *Copeia* 4.

Wigand, Peter E. 1987. "Diamond Pond, Harney County, Oregon: Vegetation History and Water Table in the Eastern Oregon Desert." *Great Basin Naturalist* 47 (3).

Williams, Howel. 1975. *The Ancient Volcanoes of Oregon*. Eugene: University of Oregon Press.

About the Author

Melvin R. Adams was born and raised in the small town of Lakeview in the desert of eastern Oregon. He spent much of his childhood outdoors, hunting, fishing, camping, and backpacking. While earning a bachelor's degree in general science at Oregon State University, he returned to eastern Oregon each summer to survey roads in the Fremont National Forest. His experiences instilled in him a love for and deep interest in the region's natural and human history.

After earning a dual master's degree in biology and geology from the University of North Dakota, Adams began a career as a science teacher. Prompted by his concern for the environment of the West, he later returned to college to study environmental engineering. He was hired at the Hanford Nuclear Reservation in the Washington desert and worked there for 24 years until his retirement.

Adams has authored or co-authored many scientific and technical papers, and published both poetry and prose. He is the author of *Netting the Sun: A Personal Geography of the Oregon Desert* (Washington State University Press, 2001). He lives in Richland, Washington, with his wife Onnie.